SUNDAY
BLOODY SUNDAY

BLAKE

Published by Blake Paperbacks Ltd
98–100 Great North Road, London N2 0NL, England

First published in Great Britain in 1992

ISBN 1–85782–018–5

British Library Cataloguing-in-Publication Data: A catalogue record
for ths book is available from the British Library

Typeset by Avocet Typesetters, Launton, Bicester

Printed by Cox and Wyman, Reading, Berkshire

Cover design by Graeme Andrew
Picture research by Martin Malin
Additional research by Peter Picton

3 5 7 9 10 8 6 4 2

To my wife Emily without whose love, help and encouragement this book and my tennis game would not have been possible.

And to my mother Mary MacKenzie who is only a phone call and 3,500 miles away from giving me some sound and loving advice.

Acknowledgements

Although it is my name on the cover, this book is really a team effort. The staff at *Sunday Magazine* came up with numerous ideas and supplied endless support and encouragement. *Sunday* Editor Sue Carroll and Deputy Editor Peter Picton deserve a special mention, but words cannot express my gratitude to Martin Malin, Karisia Cooper, Angie Mulligan, Mike Davey and Mark Lomas.

This book would have been hard to imagine without the help of dozens of detectives and prosecutors throughout the US. They gave up countless hours of their spare time to give me shocking details of these mysterious and chilling crimes.

I'd also like to give my deepest thanks to my family for their help over the years which paved the way for this book. My mother Mary MacKenzie, former deputy director of information at Greater London Council, got me out of betting shops and into the family business — journalism. My father Ian MacKenzie, retired editor of weekly papers, gave me my first job at *News Shopper*. My brother, Kelvin MacKenzie, Editor of the *Sun*, gave me my first shifts on daily papers in England and in America. My brother Craig MacKenzie, Deputy Editor of the *Sunday Express*, gave me my first freelance assignments and much advice along the way.

And I cannot forget Dick McWilliams, a producer on the American TV show A Current Affair. He always found time to help me with my crime research despite the pressures of his own job.

But most of all my heart goes out to Terri Jeffers, whose son Danny was brutally killed by her ex-husband. Her courage, as shown in this book, is an example to us all.

Drew MacKenzie has been a journalist in Britain and North America for 23 years. Starting out on weeklies in south London, he graduated to Fleet Street before emigrating to Canada where he worked for the *Hamilton Spectator* and *Toronto Star*. After moving to the US, he worked on the *Star* and then joined the *New York Post*, where he's been a senior editor for 12 years. The author has also written TV scripts for an American series and was Assistant Press and Public Relations Officer for Thorn Electrical Industries. He has a wife, Emily, and two sons, Kyle, 8, and Ross, 5.

Foreword

In these pages there are 41 shocking true-life crimes that no Hollywood scriptwriter could ever dream up. They are tales of love and lust, greed and gore, murder and mayhem. They have been giving the shudders to *Sunday Magazine* readers for two years.

Now *Sunday Magazine* has put together a collection of the most fascinating cases for its first crime book. But be warned, some of the grisly stories are so terrifying that you won't want to be home alone when you read them.

Contents

1

My Crusade for Danny Boy

They are women who share a special, bitter grief. Every one of them is a mother who has lost a little child at the hands of a murderer. The Parents of Murdered Children group, based in Houston, Texas, is battling for a compulsory death penalty for the murder of a child under six. And these grieving parents are led by a woman who has more reason than most to see child-killers executed.

Terri Jeffers, 37, was forced to listen, in horror, over the telephone as her ex-husband calmly slaughtered their three-year-old son, Danny.

The fair-haired boy had been staying with his father, carpenter Jimmy Ward, 44, for a week in August 1988, under a temporary custody deal. It was a month after Terri got a divorce from her wife-beating husband. But instead of returning him, Ward phoned Terri at her home in the quiet Houston suburb of Humble, and begged her to forgive all his brutality and come back to him.

She refused. He begged again. And again she refused. Ward began threatening to "put a bullet in Danny's head", then kill himself. Twice, he hung up.

A panic-stricken Terri phoned up Ward's mother — and the police.

The third time Ward rang, Terri had a tape-recorder tapped into the phone to collect evidence for a battle to prevent him sharing custody of the boy. And at the other end of the line, Ward had a .22 calibre hand gun, aimed at little Danny's head.

Outside, by now, Ward's mother, Margaret, was hammering on the front door. "Alright," Ward told Terri,

Jim Ward poses for a family photo with son Danny, wife Terri, and Melissa. The man Terri Jeffers thought was Mr. Perfect turned out to be a brute. But she didn't believe that he'd hurt his own boy.

his voice calm and flat, "Mum's showed up. I guess the cops will be here in a couple of minutes."

"No!" Terri lied.

"Honey," Ward told her, as the tape rolled, "I do love you."

"Don't kill my baby!" Terri pleaded. "How could you threaten to kill my baby?"

"You want to tell him goodbye?"

"You're going to kill him . . .?"

"Yes. I am. Here he is. You want to tell him goodbye?"

"Don't you dare!" the horrified Terri blustered.

"You made the decision," Ward replied in the same flat voice. "You called my bluff."

"Don't you dare touch my baby!" the mother screamed.

But the horror was reaching its climax. "Hey," Ward jeered, the gun still at his son's head, "you're the one who called in the cops. You always thought you were cool, didn't you? You did what you thought was right, huh? Think about it!"

There were two quick popping noises. Gunshots.

Terri, near collapse, managed to ring off and call the police again.

Ward had put the gun to his son's forehead, just above the little boy's right eye. And, as Danny stared up in terror at his dad, Ward fired. Then he put the gun to his own head, at the left ear, and fired again. He managed to get to the door and let his mother in before he collapsed.

Incredibly, both father and son were still alive when the ambulance came. In hospital, they were put into the same intensive care ward, just four beds apart from each other. But little Danny was already brain-dead.

He was put on a life-support system, to await the transplant team who would take his heart to save another life. Terri sat holding his hand. Danny's half-sister, Melissa, 10 — the child of Terri's first marriage — came in to say goodbye. And the killer-father was becoming conscious again . . .

* * *

3

He showed no remorse. "Get me a good cup of coffee and a good lawyer," he ordered his ex-wife. "I might get two years for this and I'll be out in about two weeks. If I have to stay in prison longer, I'll get a college degree, and get a desk job when I get out."

Terri, a lab technician, had met Ward through friends, in 1983. Like her, he had been married before. At first, she could hardly believe her luck. So soon after her first marriage had collapsed, she seemed to have found Mr Perfect.

"He seemed to be everything I wanted," she says. "A hard worker, a family man, a churchgoer. And he liked Melissa."

Within eight months, Terri knew him rather better. "He had a violent, uncontrollable temper. He'd say, 'You are never going to leave me. I'll kill you first.' He abused Melissa and me physically and emotionally. He also drank cases of beer, which made him even more vicious."

Ward was also a jealous husband. "He often accused me of being unfaithful. Once, he threatened to cut off my hands because he thought I was having an affair. Finally, I was forced to leave him.

"But he had therapy, to stop his raging tantrums, and I agreed to go back to him, for Danny's sake."

It didn't last. "His tempers started again," Terri recalls. "The final straw came when he threatened me with a gun and smashed my head against the headboard of the bed. I waited until he was out at work. Then I packed some clothes and moved into a battered wives' shelter with Melissa and Danny."

By now Danny, though only three years old, was convinced his father was going to kill him. "Danny had this premonition," Terri says. "But I just didn't take him seriously. I don't know why.

"Jim had sworn to kill me and my daughter — and even my parents — if I didn't take him back. I just never thought he'd touch Danny. Not his own son.

4

"Danny kept telling me, 'Daddy's got a gun and he's going to kill me.' And I would tell him, 'No. Daddy loves you. He's not going to hurt you.' In the final weeks before Jim did kill him, my poor little Danny was terrified."

In court, Jim Ward pleaded insanity. But he was declared fit for trial. His first wife, Geraldine Adams, mother of his two daughters, testified that his violent temper had destroyed their 11-year marriage. He once threatened to kill her, Geraldine said. "He told me he would never spend time in jail because he'd get out on the grounds of insanity."

Ward was convicted of murdering little Danny and jailed for life. But in 11 years' time, in the year 2003, he'll be eligible for parole. Terri plans to fight to keep him inside for the rest of his days. "I could never forgive him," she says. "I believe in God, but I'm angry at a God who'd let someone like Jim go up to heaven, as long as he repents."

Since Danny was murdered, his mother has carried the horrifying tape of that last phone call around in her handbag. It only lasts 30 seconds or so. But she uses it to try to persuade local politicians to vote through a new law that would bring much harsher treatment for those who kill children.

She wants any convicted child-murderer to be executed – or at the very least to spend no less than 35 years behind bars, instead of the present 15-year minimum under Texas state law. "I've got my whole life to think about this," Terri says. "It's the fire that keeps me going."

These days, Terri carries a .38 calibre gun for protection. And she has no thought of marrying again. "I live in a self-made prison," she says. "I live in fear because of Jim. And I don't think I could ever trust another man again."

Once a month, she finds solace at Parents of Murdered Children meetings. They have made a quilt with transfer pictures of their 30 dead children. At each meeting, the Keeper of the Quilt, Shirley Parish – her daughter Kimberly was killed by a madman — holds up the cloth. And one of the bereaved parents talks about the never-ending heartbreak of their loss.

Danny's picture is there on the quilt, of course. And in time, it will be Terri's turn again, to point to her little boy and tell some grieving new member about that August day in '88. The day she picked up the phone and listened to the sound of her son being murdered.

"It helps to know that others care," Terri says. "But my heart has been ripped out, just the same. All the plans I had, all the love . . . You raise your child. You teach them, you nurse them, you stay up at night when they're sick. Danny never got to play football. He never got to see the Astros baseball team. One of my last memories of him is when he was standing there in the bathtub, saying, 'I love you, Mama, I love you.' "

Terri and Melissa wrote this poem, in loving memory of their Danny:

> A million times we've missed you.
> A million times we've cried.
> If love could have saved you,
> You never would have died.
>
> Things we feel most deeply
> Are the hardest things to say.
> Our dearest one, we'll always
> Love you in a very special way.
> We often sit and think of you
> And think of how you died,
> To think we couldn't say goodbye
> Before you closed your eyes.
> No one can know our loneliness
> And no one can see us weeping.
> All our tears from aching hearts,
> While others are still sleeping.
> If we had a lifetime wish,

A dream that would come true,
We'd pray to God
With all our hearts,
For yesterday — and you.
Love, Mom and Melissa.

2

Cop by Day – Bandit by Night

Hero cop Gary Steadman, 35, got the shock of his life when he ripped the mask off a burglar he'd just shot. For it was his best friend and fellow police officer, Mike Stanewich.

Distraught Gary gently held his pal as he bled to death. He looked at Mike in disbelief and the injured man said, "Yeah, it's me Gary". When the 36-year-old stopped breathing, Gary tried mouth-to-mouth resuscitation – but it was in vain.

As other officers arrived, he cried, "I've killed my best friend. God help me, what am I going to say to his wife and kids?"

Gary and Mike had worked at the same police station in San Diego, California, for years. They went drinking together and their families were close, too. But Gary had no idea that his best buddy was a cop gone bad.

The drama began on 3 July, 1991, with a call that a house was being robbed. Gary, who was patrolling the Encinitas area of San Diego, was at the house in minutes. The burglar had beaten and threatened to kill the owner, Donald Van Ort, 32. He was handcuffed to a chair with a lighter-fuel-soaked pillow over his head.

The 6′ 3″ crook, wearing a nylon mask and rubber gloves, warned he would turn Donald into a human torch unless he opened his safe. "He said he was going to light my fire unless I gave him the combination," revealed Donald. "But I wouldn't give it to him."

The intruder had also bound and gagged Donald's grandmother Helen, 82, who was lying on a couch. "He warned me 'You're going to shut up or I'll blow your brains out,'" she said. But when Mike was clumsy enough to drop a book of matches, the elderly lady overcame her fear and hid them.

Gary burst in and shouted at the thief, "I'm a police officer, freeze!" The robber had a gun tucked in his waistband but moved towards a kitchen knife on the side of the sink. Again Gary screamed "Freeze!" But Mike still headed for the knife. Gary fired three rounds with his 9mm gun, hitting his friend twice in the back and once in the elbow.

Police now think Mike may have deliberately got himself shot because he was so ashamed at being caught as a common criminal. He was skilled in self-defence and had given lectures on how to handle encounters with armed and dangerous suspects. Captain Bon Apostolos said, "Why did he make furtive movements while standing in front of a gun? Did he want to die?"

Mike Stanewich joined the force in 1981 and rose quickly through the ranks. In 1989, the father of five was commended for "outstanding service to the community" and a year later was promoted to detective and assigned to the elite undercover narcotics unit.

Mike was well-liked at the station because of his sense of humour. And in his neighbourhood, he was a local hero who spent hours telling kids about his exploits. But there was a dark side to his character, unknown to most people.

Shortly before he became a cop, Mike was arrested in 1980 for impersonating a police officer − a fact he left off his application. A few months before he was killed he was reprimanded for the first time by his superiors, for making an unauthorised surveillance.

Mike also had money troubles. He'd been happily married to Kathy, a probation officer, for five years. They had three children − aged four, three and 22 months. Although they each earned £25,000, a new £130,000 house was draining their finances. Plus Mike had to pay £200-a-month alimony and support to his first wife and two children. His ex-wife took him to court several times after he fell behind with the payments.

Mike desperately needed cash and he knew where to get it. He was one of six plain-clothes officers who had searched Donald Van Ort's house for drugs six weeks earlier. Donald was ordered to open his safe — and all the cops had seen jewellery, heirlooms and $60,000 in cash from the sale of his grandmother's home. No drugs were discovered anywhere in the house and the police soon left.

The next day Donald saw Mike in his back yard. When confronted, the officer said he needed a urine specimen. Later Donald noticed a window had been tampered with. "I thought he was trying to plant drugs in my house," he said.

Soon after, Donald changed his safe combination and put most of the money in the bank. On the day of the robbery, Donald was in the shower when the doorbell rang. He opened the door to two men — as Mike pulled out a gun, his accomplice panicked and ran off.

Donald screamed, "It's a robbery!" — alerting his girlfriend Carla Sawcliff who was in the back room. She escaped unnoticed through a window and called the police from a neighbour's house.

Mike's car was found nearby with the plates removed, convincing detectives he'd carefully planned the whole operation. Now the police are investigating the cop's other cases to see if he returned to rob homes he'd visited during enquiries.

Donald claimed that the second thief was one of the five deputies who had swooped on his house with Mike. But the officer he picked out had an iron-clad alibi, and so did the rest of the drug squad.

Meanwhile Gary Steadman has been undergoing counselling to overcome the trauma of killing his best friend. One police official says: "Nobody feels any compassion for a crooked cop like Stanewich. I feel a lot sorrier for Gary Steadman."

3

Day I Faced Dad's Killer

John Mudd Jnr, 22, had lived with a secret so devastating, his conscious mind blotted it out for 16 years. He was only five when his adored father was murdered at home in Wilkinsburg, Pennsylvania on 28 December, 1975.

John Mudd Snr, 28 had been watching TV with his wife Arlene and their son when the TV and lights in the living room blacked out. John went down to the dark cellar to check the fuse-box.

Moments after his father had been shot seven times, the terrified little boy clearly saw the killer. But the murder was so traumatic he had erased it from his memory. It could have vanished forever, but the horror of that night came flooding back to him when, at 21, he was playing Trivial Pursuit with friends. He was about to hit a pal who'd made fun of his girlfriend, when John burst into tears. He says, "I wanted to hurt him, but went into the hallway, knelt down and everything came flooding back to me".

The drama triggered a series of clear memories which he later compared to photographic slides. But he couldn't put a name to the killer's face until police showed him a photo line-up of possible suspects.

John quickly picked out the person he'd seen after the shooting – his mother's lover, Steven Slutzker.

In 1991, he told a new inquest, "I heard seven loud noises, then I remember being at the top of the cellar steps looking down at my dad's body. I was being held by someone." He recalled sitting on the couch with his mum seeing Slutzker come out of the cellar.

Top: The horrors of the killing of his father (*pictured here*) forced all recollections of it from John Mudd's mind, until the night his memory was suddenly triggered 16 years later during a row with his friend.

Above: Amy Slutzker - testified against her father.

Top: A pal's upsetting remark while playing Trivial Pursuit, made John Jnr. recall the events of his father's murder. Here he is pictured leaving court with a friend.

Above: Steven Slutzker (left) with attourney Charles Scarlata.

It was enough for police to reopen the case and charge Slutzker, 41, with murder.

Back in 1975, police homed in on Steven Slutzker, who lived across the street. A friend of Steven's, Michael Pezzano, had told the police five days before the murder that Slutzker had tried to hire him to kill Mudd with a .32 calibre automatic gun, the same type as the murder weapon.

Police also learned that Steven and Arlene had been having an affair. They had even lived together briefly but Arlene moved back home for the sake of her young son.

At first Steven was charged with the killing, but as there was no proof he pulled the trigger, the charge was dropped. But he still faced two counts of solicitation to commit murder.

Arlene testified that the killer was probably a burglar who had entered the house through the kitchen and gone out through the cellar door. But the only footprints police found were at the front of the house. Steven's attorney suggested Arlene had killed her husband, or hired a hitman, whom she'd let out through the front door.

When Michael Pezzano testified that Steven had offered him $300 to kill John, he said "Steven wanted him killed by Christmas so that he and Arlene could have a good holiday together."

Steven was sentenced to 23 months in jail. When he walked free after a year, he thought he'd got away with murder. But he'd forgotten about the boy he thought was asleep on the fatal night.

In 1976, Arlene lost custody of John Jnr, who went to live with his aunt, Maureen Perri, near Wilkinsburg. He had no contact with his mum and grew up believing Slutzker was involved in his dad's death.

After his moment of recall, John was to get revenge on the witness stand. Psychologist Russel Scott said it was not unusual to have recall after 16 years. "When people face trauma, it can get locked in the memory but be triggered by a later event."

A surprise last-minute witness, Steven's daughter Amy, clinched the jury's verdict. Steven claimed that he and Amy had spent the night of the murder with friends.

Amy, who was six at the time of the killing, said this was a lie. She also said she had seen Steven take a gun from their dresser at home. She hadn't come forward earlier because she was terrified of her father. As a child she remembered him pulling a gun on her mother.

Arlene, called by the defence, exercised her legal right to refuse to answer questions that might incriminate her. It was revealed that Steven was an electrician, who'd installed a light in the Mudds' living room. At the time of the crime, this was the only fuse that wasn't in place − it was unscrewed.

Slutzker was found guilty and got life. The victim's sister Maureen said, "We finally got the justice due to us."

4

A Cold Killing

The last words Edward Sherman said to his pregnant wife were: "I love you, too." But a little girl who was eavesdropping on the phone thought there was something very strange about the call.

Two days later the body of Ed's wife Ellen was found in their bedroom, which was freezing cold because the killer had turned the air-conditioning up to maximum. Ellen, 38, who was five months pregnant, lay naked on the bed and had been brutally strangled with her own bikini panties. The unborn baby was also dead.

Ellen's balding husband, then 42, was ruled out as the prime suspect at the beginning because he had a concrete alibi. For Ed, a college lecturer with a genius IQ of 165, was out at sea, sailing off the coast of Maine with four friends, at the time.

When he was quizzed by the cops, he said: "I didn't kill Ellen. I'm not capable of doing such a thing. I am not a violent person. I've never hurt anyone. I just couldn't use violence on anyone."

The police began to look elsewhere for the vicious killer, but the investigation always seemed to lead back to the unfaithful husband. Police discovered that the Shermans, who had been married for 16 years, had been having angry rows over his eight-year affair with pretty Nancy Prescott.

Nancy had even given birth to Ed's daughter Rachel eight months earlier. When heartbroken Ellen found out about her husband's love-child, she got pregnant as well. Although they already had a 13-year-old daughter Jessica, Ed did not like kids, and Ellen had aborted his baby seven years earlier.

16

Nancy had also aborted Ed's child two years before she had Rachel.

Detectives also learned that Ed and Ellen had briefly separated a few weeks before the murder and then reconciled when he'd agreed to stop seeing his mistress. Ellen had threatened to kick Ed out of the house if he saw Nancy again, and warned him she'd take him to the cleaners in divorce court.

The couple were joint owners of a small advertising agency, Ad Graphics, but because she had the controlling interest and did most of the work, she'd get it if it came to a divorce battle.

On the day she was last seen it appeared that the Shermans had finally solved their marital problems because Ellen gave him a card for his 42nd birthday and a milkshake maker for a present. However, she did not know that a few days earlier Ed had tried to convince Nancy that she should leave the door open to resume the relationship "if things ever changed".

Within weeks of Ellen's death, he'd moved in with Nancy, and soon they bought a home together. Three years later, police were called to the house after he kicked her in the face. Knowing he was a murder suspect and had claimed he was not a violent person, they took photos of the bruises covering her face.

Police subsequently discovered that in 1978 Sherman had an affair with another woman whom he'd pushed into a door and then knocked down. He also tried to choke her, but she hit him over the head with a frying pan. And 19 years ago, before he met Ellen, he was briefly married. But his first wife got an annulment after he assaulted her.

Police also found a computer disk containing the manuscript of a chilling murder mystery Ellen was writing. The plot was eerily similar to real life − a wife is murdered and although her husband is the prime suspect, he was out of town at the time.

The circumstantial evidence was mounting up against Ed

but, just like in the book, he had an iron-clad alibi. Then the police heard about a TV movie called *Blackout* that Ed had seen three days before Ellen was found.

The homicide squad realised that the film probably solved their own murder case. It was a thriller about a businessman named Ed who murders his wife and then turns the air-conditioning up before going out of town.

The idea was to slow the decomposition of the body so that cops were confused about the time the wife was killed. Had Sherman also put the air-conditioning on maximum at his house in East Lyme, Connecticut, to preserve the body and mask the time of death?

The police began to think he had. They believed he'd killed Ellen early on a Friday evening and then joined his friends for a weekend sailing jaunt. The chances of proving it, however, seemed remote.

But, nearly five years after the callous crime, the police finally got their big break when Kristin McDuff mentioned to her father Henry a phone call she'd overheard around the time of the murder.

Fifteen minutes after Ed had kissed goodbye to his wife on 2 August, 1985, he stopped off to pick up Henry, who was going sailing with him. Sherman asked to use the phone so he could call his wife to tell her to shut off the battery to a sailboat they owned. Kristin, who was then eight years old and had a habit of eavesdropping, picked up the phone to make a call — unaware Sherman was using an extension in another room.

She told police: "He said, 'I love you, too' as if someone said, 'I love you' first." But all Kristin could hear on the other end was a ringing telephone.

Blonde-haired Kristin, now 15, also heard him say: "If you need anything, go to the neighbours. I have to go now."

She was ashamed about listening in on the call and for years had been afraid to tell her mother about it. "I used to listen in on my mother's conversations, then I'd feel bad," she said. It was obvious that Ed had made a fake call to

18

his wife to help prove she was still alive when he last saw her.

Sherman had also called Ellen in a ship-to-shore call, planning to tell her when he might be back and to remind her about the battery. But nobody answered. He tried again on Sunday, but still no reply.

He managed to get through to his wife's friend Barbi Lane from the ship, and asked her to check on his wife and to tell her to turn off the battery — even though he'd already told his wife that.

In March 1990, Sherman was finally charged with murder. If the foetus of his child had been three weeks older, he would also have been charged with capital murder, an offence punishable by death. The prosecution claimed he killed Ellen because she wanted him to stop seeing his lover and he faced a costly divorce if he didn't.

And the baby boy whom Ellen was carrying would have meant that he would have to spend more time at home, and thus less with Nancy and Rachel. State Attorney Robert Satti pointed out that as a Mensa member he was an intelligent person, as well as shrewd and manipulative, and was capable of planning and carrying out a murder.

Forensic tests showed that her last meal was linguini and clam sauce — which was still in her stomach, indicating she'd died from within minutes to two hours of eating on Friday night.

But the most damning evidence came from Kristin McDuff and country singer Barbi Lane, who testified that she'd spoken on the phone to Ellen on Friday morning. Lane said that Ellen was so upset about another crisis in her marriage that she couldn't talk — especially since her husband was there.

Barbi called again at 8pm that night and nobody answered. She kept on calling repeatedly for the next two days. "I was extremely upset," said Lane. She knew Ellen's daughter Jessica was away at summer camp and that Ed was off sailing, so Barbi went to Ellen's house to see if she was okay.

Lane banged on all the windows, screamed out Ellen's name and then, fearing the worst, went to get a mutual friend, Len Fredericksen, to break into the house. He recalled that the bedroom was freezing cold "like a refrigerator". He said: "I heard the air-conditioning going, so I broke in. When I got into her bedroom, it was a horrifying picture I'll never forget."

Sherman was found guilty of murder. And jury foreman Donald Arthur said: "I think it was a crime of passion and when it was over it was over."

Rose Cooper, Ellen's mother, said: "It's not bringing my daughter back, but at least there's justice."

In March this year he was sentenced to 50 years behind bars, but from the dock he continued to protest his innocence.

He said: "I want to say that I stand by my testimony. I did not kill Ellen. I don't know who killed Ellen. But I want to apologise to the woman I promised to love, honour and cherish. Each and every day for the last six years I've apologised to Ellen for the lifestyle I led. I loved Ellen but apparently I did not honour our relationship. She certainly deserved a better life than the one she lived with me. For that I'll be eternally sorry. Had we lived a better life, perhaps Ellen would have been alive today."

Then he addressed Ellen's mother, saying: "I, too, want someone punished for this crime." He also apologised to Nancy Prescott and their daughter Rachel.

He also turned to Jessica and, with tears in his eyes and a crack in his voice, said: "As I look at you, Jess, I see many of the beautiful characteristics that remind me of your mother. May God bless you."

5

Dad Forgives Daughter
for Family Slaughter

Lovely Brenda Wiley was the apple of her father's eye. The blue-eyed beauty was a bright, loving child, who never caused any trouble. And that's what made it so much harder for Mark Wiley when police told him that his wife Bonnie, 40, and son Keith, 14, had been murdered. For the unspeakable crimes had been committed by his 15-year-old daughter Brenda. Furthermore she had planned to kill her father as well.

The trouble began when Brenda suddenly blossomed into a beautiful buxom blonde. It was not long before she had a steady boyfriend, 18-year-old Keith Santana.

Three months later Brenda's lust for Keith was out of control. She'd leave her window open so he could spend passionate nights with her.

However, her parents were woken by banging noises and caught them in the act. Her dad threw Keith out of the house, in America's New Jersey, took Brenda's door off the hinges and ordered her to end the relationship. But she saw him in secret and, as a result, got grounded.

On the morning of 8 November, 1990 — the last day of her grounding — Brenda's anger suddenly boiled over.

She was cleaning the house, her brother was folding the laundry while her mother was working outside. Then her brother started calling her a sneak. She finally flipped and hit him over the head with a Pepsi Cola bottle. As he was still conscious, Brenda picked up a 10-inch-blade carving knife and attacked him in a frenzy. She stabbed him nearly 20 times, piercing his liver, heart, neck and abdomen. His last words were, "I won't tell, I won't tell."

21

She locked the door while she cleaned up the blood, and could hear her mother banging on it, trying to get in. Says Brenda: "I took this bar as my mother went round the house banging on windows. I unlocked the door and she came in. I hit her on the head. Then I took the same knife and kept hitting her. And she was dead."

Bonnie's last words to her daughter were, "What did I ever do to you?" She had 30 stab wounds and her skull was crushed by the blows.

Brenda put her brother in a sleeping bag and put a rubbish bag over his head. She mopped up before phoning Keith and telling him what she had done. Keith arrived with his friend Brian Adams and three girlfriends. While the girls waited outside, Keith and Brian went in. When they saw the grisly mess, Adams asked her why she had done it. She said she loved Keith. Then Brenda jumped into her mother's car and drove off. But her friends called the police and she was stopped.

At her trial, her lawyer Frank DiChiara claimed she was either suffering from temporary insanity or diminished capacity when she killed.

Two psychologists and a psychiatrist testified for the defence, saying she had a "severe depressive disorder" that prevented her from acting "knowingly or purposefully".

The court heard how Brenda's problems with her parents intensified when her 17-year-old brother Tim left home to enter a drug detoxification clinic.

Psychologist Dr Edward Dougherty said: "All the energy that had centred on Tim was now on Brenda." He also revealed that before killing she had twice tried to kill herself, but the gun had only fired blanks.

In her confession, Brenda said she had also planned to kill her father, but he was working at Acme's supermarket that day and so was spared.

Brenda's boyfriend testified that four days before the killings she rang him up begging him to help murder her parents. He said, "No way".

22

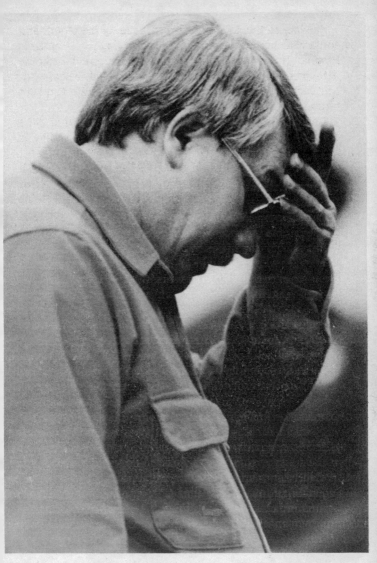

Until the day that she killed her mother and her younger brother, Brenda Wiley (pictured over) had seemed a model daughter. But when the passionate relationship with her boyfriend Keith Santana was thwarted her mood changed dramatically. Her father (above) was heartbroken.

Dr Irwin Perr, a psychologist for the prosecution, claimed that although Brenda was "thinking crazy" she was not insane.

But Brenda, now 17, claimed she was out of her mind at the time. Nonetheless, she was found guilty and sentenced to life in prison, without a chance of parole for 30 years. Her distraught father launched an appeal. He said: "She killed her own mother and brother and she was in the right frame of mind? I just can't buy that.

"Brenda is amazed I am standing by her. But I love her as much as I loved my wife and son."

6

Blind Robbery
His handicap was his fortune

Probing with a white stick in his hand, 42-year-old Bob Toe would step out of a taxi and carefully tap his way across the pavement to the bank entrance. Usually the security guard would open the door for him and then Bob would feel his way to a queue in front of a teller. When it came to his turn, Bob would hand the teller his calling card. It read: "I have a gun. Be quick, be quiet or you're dead. Put all the cash in the bag."

Seconds later Bob would retrace his steps out of the bank and hail a taxi. Because he was blind, one would usually stop for him right away. He'd tell the driver: "To the airport and step on it." Blind Bob had struck again.

Incredibly, 15-stone Robert Vernon Toe robbed 24 banks . . . despite being unable to see what he was doing. Life has been nothing more than a blur to Bob for years – but it hasn't stopped him living a successful life of crime.

Bob was born with an incurable eye disease known as *retinitis pigmentosa* – which meant as a child he could not see in the dark. Over the years his eyes gradually got worse until he became almost completely blind. "My eyes got so bad I was forced to become a crook," says Bob.

He staged his first hold-up in 1974 – just minutes after being released from prison after serving five years for a mail fraud. "I'd always wanted to be a bank robber," says Bob. "My heroes were Jesse James and Bonnie and Clyde. While I was in the slammer other cons told me there was a bank nearby nobody had ever hit, so I decided that would be my first job.

"The prison got me a cab to leave and I told the driver

to wait while picked I up some money." He certainly did – and walked out of the bank with £4,000 in a brown paper bag. He didn't even have a gun.

Three years later in New York, Blind Bob hit again. Some money he'd made as a child selling stolen fish worms vanished from his account, probably due to an accounting error. Bob was furious and got his revenge on the bank by holding it up for £1,500. "The bank guard even opened the door for me because he could see I was blind. I hopped in the waiting cab and told the driver to take me to the airport. I like New York because as soon as you stick out your hand for a cab, one stops."

Over the next few months, Bob hit another seven banks – twice he robbed two on the same day. "I'd never rob banks on a rainy day, though, because you can't catch a cab then," he says.

Barely able to make out shapes, Bob would follow people into the bank and stand in line. "Young people walk too fast so I'd always follow older ones." He'd then pass his calling card to the teller – a one-eyed jack with the message demanding money on the back.

"One time a woman started screaming in panic, so I left. I didn't want her to suffer undue stress. I pulled out my cane, walked a few blocks and robbed another bank. Then there was the time a red dye bomb went off all over the money 30 seconds after I left the bank. I was so mad I got the cabbie to take me to another of their branches and robbed that, too."

Bob was finally nabbed in 1977 by a million-to-one chance. As he unfolded his cane, he stumbled into armed guards delivering money to the bank. They were moonlighting cops – he had literally walked into the arms of the law!

Sentenced to 18 years in an Alabama jail, he was sent back to New York in 1983 for parole. But there was no halfway house that would take him, because of his handicap, and he faced another 11 years in jail. Then he got a huge break when the authorities couldn't decide where to place him so he walked free. It was the third time Bob had left prison before his sentence was finished — only the first couple of times he'd escaped.

During his first prison term, he cut through iron bars in the cell, smashed the window, cut a hole in a fence and climbed over a second barbed-wire fence. He was out for nine months before police caught up with him in Hollywood, where he'd starred in three porn movies and acted as a pimp to eight prostitutes.

"Weeks before I was finally arrested again, the FBI showed me a picture of myself and asked if I recognised this man. I couldn't see a thing so I told them I knew him but didn't know where he lived!"

After Bob was freed from jail for a third time he celebrated in his usual style — by robbing a bank. "This time I hid a Coke bottle under my coat to make it look like a shooter," says Bob, who never carried a real gun. "I got $9,000 and flew to Las Vegas." While living it up at night with leggy show-girls, Bob would commute to New York by day to do his 'job'. "I flew to New York so often I even got a frequent flyer discount from Pan Am," he laughs.

Once a little old lady tried to jump the queue Bob was standing in. "I told her to wait her turn. She wouldn't, so I said 'Dammit, lady, I'm robbing this bank'."

However, Bob's luck ran out in 1983 when he changed his routine. Instead of going back to Las Vegas, Bob went to his old neighbourhood. "The taxi driver recognised me from a wanted poster in his cab and after he dropped me off he called the cops. I was taking a stroll round my old haunts when cops armed with shotguns started following me. The first I knew about it was when they jumped on me. I crashed to the ground, shouting 'Help, help, muggers are trying to rob a blind man!' But it was no good."

Sentenced to another 17 years behind bars in Lompoc Federal Penitentiary, a maximum-security jail outside Santa

WANTED

FOR ARMED BANK ROBBERY

The above photographs depict one ROBERT VERNON TOYE, a white male, 34 years (11/25/48), 5'9", 180 lbs., brown hair, possible mustache, beard or combination of both. Subject suffers from Retinitis Pigmentosa (Night Blindness), and has diminished peripheral vision. Subject wears plain metal or black rimmed eyeglasses. Subject has numerous tattoos on his arms, chest and body. Subject seeks the company of transexuals.

Subject is armed with a handgun, and is suicidal/homicidal. APPROACH WITH EXTREME CAUTION.

Any information concerning the whereabouts of this individual should be transmitted to the Joint Bank Robbery Task Force, at 553-2816 during business hours, and 553-2700 at other times. Special Agent Henry Garcia and Detective Tom Nerney assigned.

CIRCULAR NO. 83/114
DATE PREPARED 5/13/83 | **POLICE DEPARTMENT**
CITY OF NEW YORK | LIMITED TO
DEPARTMENT
CIRCULATION

The Wanted poster that trapped Bob Toye. Jumped on by police he cried, 'Help! Muggers are robbing a blind man'.

Barbara, California, Bob made one more escape attempt in 1987.

"I climbed over two fences but set off an alarm. The guards started to come after me, so I ran — and crashed head-first into a tree, knocking myself out."

The heavily tattooed Bob admits to being a lifelong thief. He was a gang member at eight, a shoplifter at 10, a burglar at 12 and a con man at 16. "I grew up dirt-poor because my father hardly ever had work." Although he's the black sheep of the family, Bob says he's not all bad. In fact, he considers himself a modern-day Robin Hood.

He claims he's given large sums of stolen money to charities such as the Special Olympics and donated heavily to research into the eye disease *retinitis pigmentosa*. He's been paid over $17,000 for the film rights to his life story and has given it all to the RP Association. "I also get two per cent of the film's profits and plan to keep that. I'm hoping Robin Williams will play me, because I'm told we look alike and he mixes drama and comedy so well."

Meanwhile, blind Bob's life of crime is over for now — at least until his parole date in 1993. When he gets out he has a stash of cash. And where's it kept? "In the bank, of course," he laughs.

7

"Small Sacrifices"

It was a fatal attraction with a horrifying twist. Spurned Diane Downs was totally obsessed with her hunky lover Lewis Lewiston and was shattered when he ditched her.

To win him back, the 35-year-old divorcee drove her car down a deserted, wilderness road, pulled out a .22 gun and blasted away . . . at her three children sitting helplessly in the back seat.

Her seven-year-old daughter Cheryl died instantly from head wounds. Her son Danny, three, was shot in the back and is paralysed for life, and eight-year-old Christie suffered a stroke after losing several pints of blood from bullet wounds to the chest.

Dishy Diane, who was once paid $10,000 as a surrogate mother, tried to wipe out her family because Lewis hated children so much that he had a vasectomy at 21 and didn't want to be a father to her kids.

After "mommie dearest" shot herself in the arm to make it look like someone else had done it, she drove her "bleeding babies" 10 miles to the hospital to get help — for herself.

The busty blonde mail carrier told police in Eugene, Oregon, that a "deranged, shaggy-haired hitch-hiker" had shot the children. But they suspected her right from the start after she giggled in the hospital while asking them: "Is my car okay? It's brand new."

Although Christie sometimes suffers from paralysis in her arm, she recovered enough to take the witness stand a year later and testify against her murdering mother.

Evil Diane was found guilty and sentenced to life in

Top: Ann Rue, who wrote the book 'Small Sacrifices' about the Downs' case.

Above: Downs is escorted out of State Police Headquarters following her re-capture in July 1987.

prison. Now her shocking story was turned into a block-buster mini-series, *Small Sacrifices*, starring sexy superstar Farrah Fawcett with her heart-throb boyfriend Ryan O'Neal playing her screen lover Lewis.

Downs's ex-husband Steve, who is the father of the two older children, was enraged when he saw the four-hour movie. "She should have been given the electric chair — that's how it should have ended," said the dashing former model. "I'd gladly pull the switch personally.

"Dead, she'd just be a bad memory, but alive she's still a living hell that could surface and hurt the children some more."

His bitterness is an eternity away from the days when they fell in love as teenagers while going to the same school in Chandler, Arizona. Leggy Diane could not wait to leave home because she had been sexually abused by her father since she was 12. He used to take her on long, terrifying drives in the desert, while her mother was working.

Diane and Steve were married when they were both 18 and in the beginning everything was great — especially the sex.

"She was attractive with a great body, and she had the personality to match," says Steve. "And her appetite was basically insatiable — she could not get enough — with me or anyone else. Twice a night was nothing to her — she needed it much more than that. I'd go to work and I'd be beat to death. I'd wake up in the middle of the night and she'd be on top of me, going at it. Then she went on for hours on end.

"I'm not trying to make myself look a stud or anything, but my sexual appetite grew along with hers." However, their marriage started to come apart after they had had two children. He decided he didn't want any more and had a vasectomy, but the operation failed and she got pregnant again.

After he ordered her to have an abortion, she went into

34

a deep depression, realising that she desperately wanted another child. Then Steve had a second successful operation, and she decided to seduce mailman Russ Philips at the Chandler Post Office, where she worked, and have his baby instead. But her husband literally caught her in the act. "She was such a planner," Steve says with disgust. "She dropped the kids off the night before with the babysitter because, she said, she wanted to be alone with me.

"I woke up in the middle of the night and she was gone. A friend at work had told me that he'd heard my wife was fooling around with some guy in a nearby town.

"I drove down to the area and saw my wife's car there. I walked in the front door of the nearest house, which was unlocked, and began checking bedrooms. And, lo and behold, the first one I came to my wife was there naked — pumping this dude. I guess I screwed things up for them. I kicked her out of my house, but she kept begging me to come back and, and for the sake of our children, I let her."

She got pregnant by 19-year-old Russ and had his baby Danny, but kind-hearted Steve loved and treated the child like one of his own.

"I found out later that she'd had affairs with scores of men during our marriage. She went through half the mailmen where she worked, especially the married men."

Although she was an unfaithful wife, Diane appeared to be a loving mother. "The children adored her," adds Steve. "They had a special attachment to her. She put up a complete facade of being a nurturing mother."

But there were early signs that Diane, who had slashed her wrists as a teenager, was a time-bomb waiting to explode.

"She could be pretty weird at times. She would turn against herself and scream her lungs out. She'd get so tense that she would just lie on the floor and be as stiff as a board. She'd scratch her face with her nails while being careful not to draw blood or scar herself. That always kind of scared me. Who would do that to themselves?

"But I was not a professional, so there was no way I could

tell that I'd married a monster in the making. We finally got a divorce when she got my oldest daughter to lie about where she was while she was out having an affair.''

After they split, Diane moved into a mobile home and was desperately short of cash. She saw a TV show about surrogate mothers and offered her services to a local agency that paid $10,000 a birth.

But at first she was rejected as being mentally unstable because she showed signs of psychopathic behaviour, and it was feared that she was unlikely to give up the child.

On the second attempt, doctors gave her a clean bill of health and she was inseminated with sperm from a donor, in the next room.

She gave birth to a healthy baby girl and gave her a big hug before signing away all rights to the child. Nobody knows if the girl's parents are aware that the real mother of their child is a sick, sex-mad child-killer.

It was about this time that she fell in love with lusty Lewis at the post office, where she wore cut-off T-shirts and no bra to turn him on. He said: ''Our affair began when she told me she was afraid of having any more affairs with married men because she'd get pregnant.

''I asked her why she didn't have an affair with someone who wouldn't get her pregnant. She said, 'Like who?' and I said, 'Like me.'

''I expected a short-term, easy-going thing like the flings I had during my first marriage, but it went on and on. My wife Nora wasn't home till five, so I had lots of time in the afternoon. She suspected something, but I lied to her all the time and told her nothing was going on.''

He finally dumped Diane after he found out that she'd given him venereal disease. He told his wife all about it and she forgave him. ''I took Nora, on my birthday, to a clinic for treatment. It was so humiliating.''

Although Diane had seduced many men, she was now besotted with only one, and wasn't going to let go of him easily. She found more ecstasy in their lovemaking than she'd known with any of her lovers. So she bombarded Lewis with love letters and poems, and begged him to leave his wife. When he refused, she moved with her children to Oregon, thousands of miles away, hoping in vain that he would follow her. As the months went by, she grew more convinced her children were to blame for the break-up.

Says Steve: "She told me a number of times that Lewis hated kids. She said that, if she didn't have kids, there wouldn't be a problem between them."

In the months after the shooting, as police built their case against her, she began hitting the bottle hard. In her diary, she wrote: "I've been drinking a lot in the past few days. I just wish I could be dead, but I had a great idea. Tell ya later if it works."

Because she dearly missed the children she had shot in cold blood, she wanted to get pregnant again. In a drunken stupor, she called an old friend, Matt, and invited herself over. An angry Matt says: "She walks in with a six-pack of beer and says, 'Guess what? I'm on birth control pills now.' I guess I was a damn fool. I was set up. It wasn't a seduction; it was a manipulation. She was using me."

But Diane was overjoyed with her sixth pregnancy and proudly told a TV interviewer at the time: "You can't replace children but you can replace the effect they give you.

"They give me a reason to live and a reason to be happy. And that's gone. They took it from me. But children are so easy to conceive." She was eight months pregnant when she was finally charged with the horrendous crime of shooting her own children.

Her baby Amy Elizabeth was taken away from her by the State immediately after the birth and given up for adoption. Her other two children, Christie and Danny, were adopted by Fred Hugi, the prosecutor who sent her to jail for life. Their real fathers have not seen them in six years. Steve,

35, who is happily remarried, says: "I really miss them and love them, but I couldn't afford their health bills.

"It was better that Fred took them. He's a wonderful man, and they are now in safe hands. He'll never let my ex-wife harm them again."

Diane has always professed her innocence, not flinching from her story about the hitch-hiker who shot her kids because she wouldn't give him the car keys. But she was found guilty on all counts and jailed at the minimum-security Oregon Women's Corrections Centre, which she escaped from three years ago.

After she'd climbed over the fence and done a runner, a massive dragnet was launched while her children were in protective custody 100 miles away. It was 11 days before the FBI tracked her down to a seedy little house less than half-a-mile from the prison.

Three men were arrested for harbouring an escaped convict — one of whom, Wayne Seifer, was the husband of Diane's cellmate Louise. She broke down and wept in jail as he admitted on TV that he'd fallen in love and slept with Diane in their short time together.

Said Wayne: "I've told her, 'I'll take care of you and when you feel you have to leave, you have to leave.' Diane was the most honest woman I've ever known."

Her murder trial had gripped the north-eastern states and the public fully expected that fertile Diane would be pregnant by Wayne. To her disappointment, she wasn't.

Diane is now in a maximum-security prison in New Jersey and is not due for parole until 2014. Farrah, who plays Downs in the mini-series, at first turned down the role because she was sickened by the thought of playing such a despicable woman.

"For a woman to kill is unbelievable," says the real-life mother of Ryan's child Redmond. "For a woman to kill her children is unspeakable. I really didn't want to do it. I didn't like the woman and didn't think I could do it justice. Diane was diagnosed as being histrionic, narcissistic and a sociopath. I'm not used to playing a character that I don't identify with in some way. But something drew me to her, although she was in no way vulnerable or sympathetic. And in the end I thought it was my best work. For the first time in my career I could be uninhibited. It was easy for me because, except for the crime, Diane was a good-time girl who liked to party, to drink, and liked men.''

8

The Nastiest Nice Guy of All

When Vietnam vet Arthur Shawcross pedalled down the street on his bike, people would wave or stop him for a chat. He was the neighbourhood nice guy who baked pies and cookies for the elderly and gave out gifts to friends, especially women. He once handed out clothing to a family whose house had burned down, and he cheerfully ran errands for his wife. But little did the locals know that the soft-spoken Shawcross was still on parole after spending 14 years in jail for raping and killing an eight-year-old girl. And so it came as an even bigger shock to the community when he was suddenly charged with being a brutal mass murderer.

His wife Rosemary, who'd been his prison pen-pal and knew of his violent history, has refused to see him since his arrest but his mistress Carla Neal still loves him — although she could have one day become one of his victims. "No matter what happens, I'll be there for him," says the 58-year-old cook, who had an affair with him for two years. "I'm too deeply in love to do anything to hurt him. He may have done wrong, but he treated me better and he treated me with more respect than my children's father ever did. They'll send him back to prison but, with God's help, I'll go see him wherever he goes." Mother-of-ten Carla is angry at his wife for not sticking by him or going to see him. "She hasn't written him a letter or even asked how he's doing."

She revealed to the cops that Shawcross would express outrage at the killings when he was reading about them in the local paper and he would warn her to be careful. "He'd say: 'When is this going to stop? Every few days they find a body. I don't want you to be out on the streets alone.' "

Police in Rochester, New York, a town of 240,000, grilled the 58-year-old grandmother about Shawcross, but she says: "I told them all I know because I didn't know anything bad about him." Her help, however, was crucial in linking him to the slaughter. She took cops to Shawcross's favourite fishing haunts along the Genesee River and it turned out that several murdered women were found in the same remote area, not far from the local red-light district. The police also found an earring in Carla's car that matched an earring worn by one of the victims. She added that when she asked him during the jail visit why he did it, "he just looked at me with passionate eyes and said, 'I don't know.' "

But Shawcross was always a violent person – at school he beat up smaller kids. He was often in scrapes with the law and was arrested for shoplifting and starting a blaze at a milk plant where he worked. After he served in Vietnam, he was jailed for two years on burglary charges and was paroled in 1971. The next year, he was convicted of strangling eight-year-old Karen Hill and dumping her body under a bridge. He returned the day after killing her and ate an ice-cream near her body. He also admitted the horrifying murder of 10-year-old Jack Blake, who vanished from his home during a robbery. Shawcross told a psychiatrist that he killed Karen because she reminded him of his younger sister Jeannie, with whom he'd had sexual relations as a child. He said: "One day I was fishing and I was thinking about Jeannie and this girl showed up. It was at that moment that I didn't hear nothing around me, and daylight got brighter, and I just grabbed this girl. All I could see was Jeannie. And I strangled her, and I raped her."

When he was paroled in 1987 after 15 years in jail, Shawcross went back to New Delhi, in New York State, but a furore erupted among townsfolk who feared for their children's lives. The same thing happened when he moved to nearby Binghampton. Police hassled him every day until he finally moved to Rochester with his prison pen-pal Rose, whom he took for his fourth wife even though he was already carrying on an affair with Carla at the time.

When killers are freed from jail, statistics show that they are highly unlikely to kill again – only a one in 20 chance of that happening. So it was no surprise that Shawcross's parole officer did not suspect him of the shocking string of murders that began in March the next year – especially since he only rode a bicycle. He was viewed as a paedophile, not a man who attacked call girls.

"Serial killers are extremely ordinary and blend in very well," said Dr James Fox, a US university criminologist and author of a book on mass murder. "They're not glassy-eyed lunatics."

The balding and paunchy Shawcross took a night job as a three-dollar-an-hour salad maker for a food wholesaler and spent his spare time fishing. Unknown to his wife he took up another hobby . . . going to hookers. He was a popular customer, giving some of them bags of fruit or potatoes and paying $15 more than their usual $35 rate. Then they started disappearing, one by one. But police did not admit to the press that a "Yorkshire Ripper" style killer was at large until two months before Shawcross was arrested.

He'd pick them up in Carla's car and take them down to the river for sex. Afterwards he'd strangle or suffocate them or just beat them to death. Some of them he killed after they ridiculed him because he appeared impotent. He cut open one victim, 20-year-old June Stott, from her neck to her pelvis and covered her with pieces of carpet to hide the body. One woman was murdered after telling Shawcross that she was not a prostitute and, in fact, was a virgin. Another was killed when she accidentally damaged the knob on the gear stick of his girlfriend's car. He also killed a second mistress in a rage after she punched him while they were swimming in the river. Police claimed that he had planned to kill 59-year-old Dorothy Keeler anyway after she'd threatened to tell his wife about their affair. He cut off her head and police were not able to identify her body until Shawcross was charged. His other victims were Dorothy Blackburn, 27, Patricia Ives, 25, Frances Brown, 22, Anne Steffen, 27, Darlene Trippi, 32, Maria Welch, 22, Felicia Stephens, 20, Elizabeth Gibson, 29, and June Cicero, 34.

His two-year reign of terror came to a sudden end with an incredible stroke of luck. Three alert state troopers were flying in a helicopter over dense woods, hunting for a missing hooker, when they spotted a man eating a salad lunch while sitting in a Chevrolet car on top of a bridge. When they also noticed a woman's body under the viaduct, they followed the car to a nursing home where Shawcross's wife worked. He was questioned briefly by police on the ground and released until the next morning, when another prostitute was found dead just two miles from the bridge. He admitted all the killings and even told police where they could find three more bodies. During his confession, he said he killed one after she bit him, another for being too loud during intercourse, another for trying to steal his wallet, and a fourth for calling him a "wimp".

In a letter to a psychiatrist, full of bad spellings and missing words, sinister Shawcross said: "I should be castrated or have an electrode placed in my head. I'm just a lost soul looking for release of my madness. Please God, let someone help me." He claimed at his trial that he was innocent − by reason of insanity because he was brain-damaged and had multiple personalities, including himself as a child, his mother, his sister Jeannie, and a man from a former life. The jury was shown a shocking video of Shawcross under hypnosis, during which he told horrifying stories of cannibalism, mutilation, child abuse and incest. Sometimes crying as he spoke, he said he was sexually molested as a child by his mother, who stuck a broom up his backside or gave him enemas for being naughty. He said his mum burned his fingers on the stove as a punishment for stealing, and threatened him with a knife when she caught him playing with himself. Identifying himself as his mother Bessie, he took on a falsetto voice and said: "I keep trying to get him to stay away from these girls and he won't listen. They ain't nothing but trouble, but he never learned." He suggested that his mother had somehow taken control of him during the murders, but the prosecution claimed he was modelling himself after Norman Bates in the *Psycho* movie to avoid jail.

As himself under hypnosis he described how he killed June Stott, a friend whom he'd often met for coffee. On the day she died, she asked Shawcross to show her how to make love but then threatened to tell police he had raped her. "Then some sensation came over me," he recalled. "I start sweating like crazy, and the daylight around me got brighter and brighter, and I didn't even hear the birds or anything around me. I'm there but I'm not there. I just grabbed her around the neck, but it was like I was standing there watching someone else do it. I don't hear nothing − not a bird, not an insect, not a plane, not even the wind. And I'm soaking wet." When he killed June Cicero, he again felt like someone else was carrying out the heinous act. "I get a feeling in me that I'm not alone in the car with her. Then I feel like I'm floating away. I'm not even in the car, but I can see in the car."

He claimed that he ate parts of two women he killed and that he also cannibalised two Vietnamese women while in Vietnam. Police denied he ate his victims and the army said he had a non-combat role in the war and so was unlikely to have had a chance to eat corpses. Under hypnosis, he also took on the personality of a friend called Ariemes from a previous life, who had watched over him since he was nine. Saying he first learned to eat flesh during medieval times in England, he said that Ariemes was with him when he killed Jack Blake. His defence lawyers claimed that Shawcross had a hole in his brain and that he suffered from post-traumatic stress disorder caused by severe child abuse.

But the prosecutor alleged Shawcross dreamed it all up

and the jury agreed with him. They found him guilty of first-degree murder and he was sentenced to 250 years in jail. Karen Hill's father Robert was delighted, saying: "They should have hung him in 1972. I now hope they put him in an electric chair with double voltage and ampage because that's what he deserves." However, they do not have the death penalty in New York State, so Shawcross will rot in jail for the rest of his life. But Carla will be able to see him once a month.

"I'll be there," she vows.

9

Die, Daughter, Die

Grocer Zein Isa, 60, and his wife Maria, 48, were sure they could get away with murder when they repeatedly stabbed their rebellious daughter to death. But, unbeknown to them, they were being recorded by government agents who were investigating them as possible spies.

The savage couple were furious with their 16-year-old daughter Tina for sleeping with a black man, staying out late and working in a fast-food restaurant.

When her boyfriend, 20-year-old Cliff Walker, walked her home at midnight one evening, it was the last straw and her parents decided to kill their wild child.

Hidden bugs linked to tape recorders picked up the shocking last minutes of Tina's life, as she kissed Cliff goodnight and went inside.

"Where have you been?" screamed her mother. Tina told her she had been working her first shift at Wendy's restaurant. "We don't accept you working," yelled her father.

The bitter conversation grew louder and louder as her parents raged about Tina taking a job and having a black boyfriend.

"I know you're trying to throw me out, aren't you?" said Tina. Her father called her a she-devil and she said she was going to leave home.

Zein said: "Do you know that this is your last day? That you are going to die tonight?"

Then on another chilling tape, picked up by a bug in another room, there are sounds of a struggle. Tina is heard screaming again and again — each time sounding more desperate. But her father just says, "Keep still, Tina."

Between her shrieking and crying, Tina begs, "Mother, please help!" Maria replies, "Are you going to listen?" Tina, "Yes, yes, yes I am." Maria yells "Shut up."

Seconds later Zein says, "Die, die quickly. Die, my daughter, die." Her screams then slowly subside, turning into barely audible groans and laboured breaths before Tina finally becomes silent.

Tina died of six to eight stab wounds in the chest from a black-handled boning knife. Her father called the police, telling them he had acted in self-defence after his daughter had demanded £2,500 and attacked him with a knife.

Zein knew his wife and his three other children would support him and he fully expected to go free. But he hadn't bargained on the tapes.

He was a Palestinian from the trouble-torn West Bank in Israel and had come to America looking for a better life. He married Brazilian beauty Maria and they had four daughters. And although Maria was a Catholic, he brought up the children in his strict Islamic faith.

Zein eventually became an American citizen and opened his own successful grocery store in St Louis, Missouri. But the FBI believed he was working for the Palestine Liberation Organisation and planted electronic monitoring devices in his home. They had been bugging his house for three months before that fateful night on 7 November, 1989.

As Zein and Maria spoke poor English, the recordings had to be translated from his Arabic, his wife's Portuguese and the little English they both knew.

The FBI handed over the shocking tapes to the police. Zein tried to have them suppressed from evidence by claiming they were unlawfully authorised under the Foreign Intelligence Surveillance Act. And, although he had been to Israel three times in the past five years, he claimed he had no links with the PLO.

But Judge Robert Gibson said: "The court was convinced that overwhelming support existed for issuing a surveillance

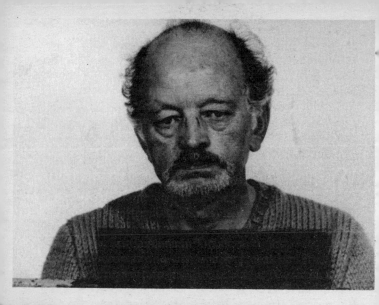

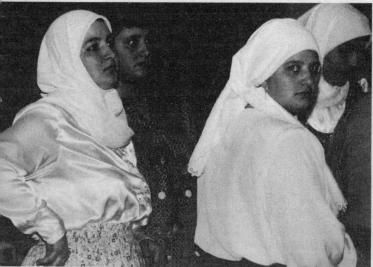

Top: While her mother held her down, Tina Isa was knifed by her father Zein Isa (*pictured here*) in the chest.

Above: Tina's sisters, Fatima, Soraia and Azizah supported their parents' beliefs and acted in accordance with ancient laws.

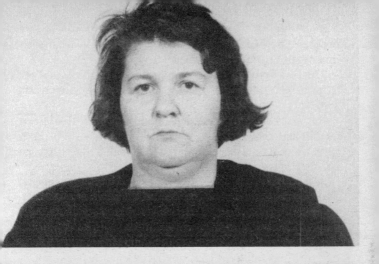

Murdered By Her Dad - Beautiful 16 year old Tina, (*above*,) had her whole life in front of her until her fanatical father Zein sa, helped by her mum, Maria, (*top*,) decided to cut it short. Together they planned the ultimate punishment for their 'rebel' child. The ruthless parents stabbed her to death.

order." The FBI have refused to comment on what their investigation of Zein revealed.

The Isas were charged with murder and while Zein stuck to his defence claim, his wife alleged she was trying to protect Tina.

But once again the hidden tapes – this time of their telephone conversations – were their downfall. They revealed that the Isas had plotted to kill Tina in revenge for her disgracing the family honour.

Although Maria was a Catholic, her three older daughters, Fatima, Soraia and Azizah, had stuck to the ways of Islam. But Tina, whose full name was Palestina, rebelled against the rigid Arab family rules.

She wore tight jeans and put on make-up when she went out with her hunky, black boyfriend.

The clash of cultures led to violent family fights, with Tina going to school with black eyes and her body covered in bruises.

At the murder trial, Zein's lawyer told the jury: "Tina had developed an absolute hatred of her father and had threatened him several times."

Zein took the stand and testified in Arabic that the bugs dotted around his house hadn't picked up his daughter's demand for cash to leave home. He also explained that he told her she was "going to die tonight" because she "already had the knife in her hand". He said, "I then directed the knife towards her to stab her until she fell down". Zein said that Tina got the knife, not him. "I didn't attack her. She went to the kitchen and came back so fast."

Isa said he'd struggled with Tina on the floor and at one point put his foot in her mouth to muffle her screams and stabbed her some more.

He pointed out that he'd once had to call police to his store after Tina tried to hit him with a can and threatened him with a meat cleaver. "She never showed me any respect," he said. "If I asked her to bring me a cup of coffee or a glass of water she would kick me in my bad leg."

Zein alleged that he had never objected to Tina having a black boyfriend and that he'd even offered them money to help get them started in married life. But prosecutors maintained that tapes from the bugged phone revealed it was not a self-defence or spontaneous killing.

For months before the murder Zein told friends and relatives that Tina was beyond redemption and had discussed different ways of killing her without him being charged with murder. On one tape, he said: "For me this has become a burned woman, a black whore and there is no way to cleanse her except through the red colour that cleanses her."

And when his married daughter Fatima Abdejabbar called to urge him to be strict with Tina, he said: "If God makes my wish, I'll put her in the grave. I'll put a knife in her hand after she falls down, of course."

Fatima even offered a curse of her own for Tina. "May God pain her, may God make her sleep and not get up. She is a whore. She will never enter my house."

The next day his other married daughter Soraia phoned to suggest that Tina be chained up in the basement and her passport be sent to the homeland. Zein replied he'd have to send Tina "home in a box".

Soraia told him if he killed Tina the family would defend him, saying that he had acted in accordance with the ancient laws of his homeland.

Defence lawyers claimed that the only crime that Maria committed was being married to Zein, who during his testimony begged the court to have mercy on his wife. "Punish me the way you want," he said. "My wife has nothing to do with it."

But prosecutor Robert Craddick proved that she took an active part in the killing by pointing out that Tina was a " strong, vigorous young woman". She was about the same size as her father, and he needed his 15-stone wife to pin their daughter to the floor while he killed her.

Medical evidence showed that Maria held Tina down by her hair, although she said she was just trying to pull her away in the struggle. But pathologists pointed out that without Maria's help, Zein wouldn't have been able to stab Tina repeatedly in the chest. His daughter would have fought and been stabbed in other places.

Although the FBI tapes showed Maria had often sided with Tina in domestic disputes, the prosecution argued that she'd help kill her because of the black boyfriend.

Tina's school guidance counsellor Pamela Fournier testified that after a stormy meeting with Maria, she had told the headmaster that the family "was going to stone that girl".

Fournier also said that Maria told her she was keeping Tina from school as punishment for going out with Walker, whom she'd been seeing for nine months.

Walker told the jury that when he walked Tina home that night, she told him that she expected a family fight. "She told me that if I heard screaming she would come back out. But she never did and I left."

But it was the gruesome tapes of Tina's murder that convinced the jury of the Isas' guilt. Zein and Maria were found guilty of first-degree murder this year and the jury recommended that they be executed. The husband and wife are now waiting to learn their fate.

Their other daughters, however, still stick by them. "There is no justice," says Fatima. "The only reason this happened is that my father is Palestinian. I do not feel sorry for my sister, I only feel sorry for my parents."

10

Double Jeopardy

Landlord Russell Swart shocked a packed courtroom when he confessed to strangling his sexy tenant Julie Everson. He dropped his bombshell just as his best friend Keith Bullock – who pleaded guilty to killing Julie – was about to be sentenced for the hideous crime.

After Swart, made his confession, he walked out of the court as free as a bird. The charges against Bullock were quickly dropped and he was also a free man.

Two men had admitted to killing Julie, but nobody would ever go to jail for it. Swart and Bullock had reason to rejoice, but only one of them had reason to laugh at the law. For he'd just got away with murder. The sensational case shocked the whole of America and left Julie's angry family wondering whether there was any justice in the world.

The Eversons' nightmare began on 28 December, 1990 when Bullock was arrested for assaulting Julie, his 29-year-old girlfriend. Swart paid Bullock's bail so he remained free until the trial.

Everson and Bullock were living together in an upstairs flat of a large house at 3027 Clinton Avenue, Minneapolis, which was owned by Swart. Their relationship had often been stormy, with many fights. Julie also had several angry rows with her landlord, who lived downstairs, and she once called the police to have Swart removed from her flat after he'd refused to leave.

On 29 December, Julie did not show up at the supermarket where she worked as a cashier. Then the battery charges against Bullock, 28, were dropped when she failed to appear in court to testify against him.

After Julie had been missing for a few days, her distraught mother Joan went to the police. Believing a frightened Julie had run away from Bullock, the missing persons bureau said there was little they could do.

Mrs Everson tried to get into Julie's flat to see if there were any clues to her whereabouts, but Swart refused to let her in. He even threatened to have her charged with stealing her daughter's belongings.

As days stretched into weeks and then months, mother-of-six Joan finally went to the homicide division and begged detectives to investigate the case. She pointed out that Julie had been having bitter arguments with both her boyfriend and her landlord just before she'd disappeared. Armed with a search warrant, detective lieutenant Charlie Miles and a team of officers went over Swart's house with a fine-tooth comb. But they found nothing.

Then the cops looked in the backyard, where they noticed there was a large mound of dirt as well as a depression in the ground. There, buried three foot down, was Julie's nude body. Her mouth and nose were covered with duct tape and her head was covered with plastic. Her legs and hands were also wrapped in tape – and she had been strangled.

Swart and Bullock were arrested and charged with second-degree murder with intent. But under Minnesota state law, they had to be tried separately. Swart, who claimed he was innocent, was set for trial first. He was tried just before Christmas, when jurors are notoriously more interested in buying presents than serving justice.

The jury decided that there was insufficient evidence to find Swart guilty "beyond a reasonable doubt" of killing Julie. And he went home a free man.

Five months later it was Bullock's turn in the dock. But prosecutors managed to talk him into accepting a plea bargain – admitting to second-degree murder committed during a felony offence. By pleading guilty to a lesser charge, he would have served 12 years in jail – or eight years with parole. If he'd been convicted of murder with intent, he'd have faced 30 years in jail — or 20 years with parole.

Bullock told relatives he believed there was a good chance he'd be found guilty of murder with intent because he'd beaten Julie up the day she'd disappeared. Also, Swart had already been found innocent and, therefore, Bullock was the only other person who was likely to have killed her.

The prosecution, however, should have known his confession was false. For Bullock claimed he'd smothered Julie with a pillow, which police knew could not be true. She had died of strangulation, not asphyxiation.

After being granted immunity from further charges, Swart agreed to testify on behalf of the prosecution at Bullock's pre-sentence hearing. But instead of helping to put his friend behind bars for a long time, Swart helped Bullock to go free as well. At Swart's own trial he'd professed his innocence but at Bullock's trial he admitted killing Julie. Swart, a burly six-foot nightclub bouncer, told the court that Julie had planned to move out after her fight with Bullock, and he went upstairs to check if she'd left.

He said: "When I got to the top of the stairs, I saw Julie in the bathroom. She started hollering at me to get out and leave her alone. She flipped out. She caught me off-guard. She cut me on the hand.

"I grabbed her with my left hand by the throat. She was berserk. I picked her up to restrain her and then she was dead. My only intent was to restrain her. I didn't realise that I would kill her."

He carried her body into the garage where he left it for four months, until the ground outside thawed and he could bury her in a shallow grave. When he ended his confession, Julie's sister Jill suddenly sprang out of her seat and screamed: "You son of a bitch. You killed her and you got off. Someone ought to kill you."

Because Swart had already been acquitted of killing Julie,

he could not be tried for her murder a second time. Under the US Constitution it's the law to prevent what's known as "double jeopardy".

Famed American civil rights attorney William Kunstler said: "Swart could have come out of that courthouse following his acquittal and screamed to the high skies that he was guilty, and there's not one thing that anyone could do against him then or now."

Richard Frase, University of Minnesota law professor, said: "The point of this law is to protect the accused from having to defend themselves over and over again. If prosecutors are allowed repeated attempts to try the same case before one jury after another, there's a likelihood they will find a jury willing to convict."

Pete Connors, the county attorney who prosecuted both Swart and Bullock, was furious with the confession, even though it meant an innocent man had escaped jail. He said: "Sometimes our system of justice lets the guilty go free. Our founding fathers recognised that. We are happy about finding the truth, but are we happy about Mr Swart walking free? Absolutely not.

"I hope in the end there will be some form of justice for the Eversons. I recognise that Julie's family and friends are devastated to find out Swart is the killer."

Connors said he was "convinced" that Swart's story was the truth and that he had not concocted a lie with Bullock to have him cleared as well. But Julie's sister Jill believes Swart lied when he said that he'd killed Julie in self-defence. Said Jill: "I think he went up there to kill her. He wanted her dead."

Julie's father Gerry said: "It's a travesty of justice. I knew Swart was guilty the whole time. This man admitted he killed her, yet he gets off without any punishment. It's the most outrageous and ridiculous thing I've ever seen. If I arranged for someone to kill him for murdering my daughter, I'd be put in jail for a very long time."

And Julie's mother Joan added: "There's something

wrong with the system. Is the loss of a kid so very hard to understand?"

The mother-of-six added that she had talked to lawyers about bringing a civil suit against Swart. "We have to do something because of what's going on in this country. Maybe a lawsuit will set a precedent. Maybe it will help other people in a similar situation."

But the Bullock family was delighted. "It was like winning the lottery," said his father Douglas, adding that the family planned to "baby" Keith for a while. Bullock had spent 10 months in jail waiting for trial. Keith's sister Kathy Long said that the fact he was learning disabled led to the false statements her brother gave to the police about how and when Julie had died.

She said: "Keith couldn't see the whole picture. His capacity for understanding events as they happen is what other people have." His brother Mark said that Keith, a restaurant busboy, was so naive that he was "convinced there was enough evidence to put him away".

Mark added: "We told him we didn't want him to go away for 30 years, and to take the plea bargain. We believed him innocent, but we wanted him home in eight years.

"Keith told me, 'I'm going to go with the plea bargain, but I don't want you to think I did it because I'm saying I did it'. "

Swart's attorney Peter Wold said that his client had "always wanted" to tell the truth about how Julie died but wasn't willing to do so unless he was granted absolute immunity.

Wold explained that although Swart could not be tried for murder again, he could be prosecuted under federal law for violating Julie's civil rights. Wold said: "I had to make sure his rights were protected. When he was given immunity, he testified to the whole truth."

Double jeopardy means Swart is literally getting away with murder. But an editorial in the local paper, the *St*

Paul Pioneer Press, believes that justice will eventually be served.

It said: "At the very heart of the American criminal justice system lies this principle: it is better for the guilty to go free than the innocent to be punished. Mr Bullock is restored to his family and his life. While Mr Swart cheated justice and should be in prison, we take comfort in the knowledge that conscience is a more tireless pursuer."

11

Mr Bigamy
He said "I do" 105 times

Would you marry this man? Well, 105 women said yes,
putting Giovanni Vigliotto in the *Guinness Book of Records*
for bigamy. He was so carried away with his new loves, he
forgot to divorce their predecessors. Or was he?

His career took him right round the world. And netted
him a fortune. The "Italian Stallion" walked 105 women
down the aisle – an average of one every four months.
There were weddings in 26 American states and 15 other
countries. He used 50 aliases – so it's not surprising he
couldn't remember them all. "I didn't keep score," he
explained.

Giovanni's only legal wife is believed to have been Joan
Bills, whom he married in Korea in 1949, when he was 19.
Three years later the bigamy spree got under way . . .

A couple of ceremonies at Houston, Texas, in 1952 turned
Ann Hendrix and Margie Lang into the first of the bogus
Mrs.Vigliottos. Next year Giovanni was back in Korea,
wedding Mi Wha Hann Chuchon. A few months later he
married Shizuko Yamaguchi in Japan. Then it was on to
Hong Kong and the charms of Sue Ming.

Giovanni got hitched twice in London in 1966, to Betty
Hume and Dinah Smathers. In 1968, he plucked four more
"wives" off one loveboat cruise on the SS *Mariposa*.

Vigliotto was tall, distinguished and seemingly rich. But,
"As a stud, he was a dud," said wife 104 Sharon Clark.
"Although he could charm the tail off a rattlesnake."

The supercharmer claimed: "I'm in love with life, women,
marriage." But he was much more in love with money. The
love 'em, loot 'em Lothario prowled flea markets, eyeing

Heartbreaker Giovanni Vigliotto, a.k.a. Fred Jipp, at the end of his 105-bride spree. 'I'm in love with life, women, marriage' he said - and cash.

Top left: Pat Gardiner, No.105. 'He'd wake me at night and say sweet things.'

Top right : Sharon Clark, No.104. 'He was a dud as a stud but a convincing charmer.'

Above: Joan Bacarella - 'He wrote me poetry and bought me flowers.'

up the stall-holders or shop owners. He wined and dined them, talked them into a quickie wedding and asked them to let him handle their money. Then he vanished.

"Giovanni promised me love and devotion" said Joan Bacarella, 50, of New Jersey, who met him after her marriage failed. "He seemed so sensitive. He wrote me poetry and bought me big bunches of flowers."

Joan was one who didn't "marry" Giovanni. But she was ripped off for £20,000. She sold her house and her clothes store − then let him drive off to sell her belongings, leaving Joan and her three kids destitute.

His final victim, No 105, was estate agent Pat Gardiner, 50, of Mesa, Arizona, who lost £18,000. "He became the husband I wanted," she said. "He'd wake me in the night and say sweet things."

Pat, too, sold her house for Giovanni. They also loaded everything into a van and drove to Palm Springs, California. There, he abandoned her in a motel with her dog, Mindy, while he went off to sell the goods for her. "I'll never trust any man again," Pat said.

Just before meeting Pat, Giovanni married divorced antique dealer Sharon Clark in 1981. "He excited me," she said. "He had style. But he was a kinky, weird lover. He asked me to rip off his clothes because they were given to him by other women. He called me a witch."

After a hippie-style wedding in the Tennessee hills, Giovanni persuaded Sharon to sell her house − and her mother's too, then hand him the money to invest. She also let him drive off with antiques worth £25,000.

But Sharon swore revenge. She and a man friend went on a hunt, following a map on which Giovanni had marked flea market towns. "I kept coming across my things that he'd stolen," she said. After six months, in Panama City, Florida, Sharon saw him getting out of a car. "My friend slashed his tyres and I called the police. They came just in time."

Giovanni − police say his real name was Frederick

Bertram Jipp — was jailed for 34 years in 1982, for bigamy and fraud. "I hope he dies inside," a bitter Pat Gardiner said.

In February 1991 she got her wish. Giovanni died of a brain haemorrhage in Arizona State Prison. None of his 100-plus widows went to the funeral. But there was still a woman at his side: private eye Pat O'Connor, who'd fought to free him. "He was a genius," she said. "No wonder so many women fell in love with him."

12

Cold Comfort

Housewife Irene Avila was devastated when her beautiful teenage daughter Missy was found brutally murdered with her hair hacked off. The divorced mother-of-four needed someone's shoulder to cry on, someone whom she could pour out her heartache to.

Missy's best friend Karen Severson saw the intense emotional pain Irene was going through, and so two weeks after the killing she moved in with the Avila family to help console them. Karen, 17, who lived just down the street, stayed for nearly two months — sleeping in Missy's bed. She even joined the Avilas for their first Thanksgiving dinner without Missy.

"She was there to comfort me," said 47-year-old Irene. "She used to see me every day and saw what hell I was going through. She became like part of the family. She was close to me like another daughter."

Severson also appeared to be deeply affected by the loss. She often took flowers to the cemetery, wrote letters to Missy and brought a Christmas tree to the grave. She also carved a note on a tree near the murder scene saying: "Missy & Karen 4 Ever."

They were very close, though to look at they were exact opposites. Slim and pretty, the vivacious 17-year-old Missy, 5ft 2in tall and weighing under seven stone was popular with boys and made friends easily. Karen, on the other hand, was unattractive and overweight, and she was known to have a big mouth and was always getting into fights.

After the murder, she really packed on the pounds, ballooning to 14 stone. "She started drinking a lot," says

Irene. "When I asked her why, she said it was because she'd lost her best friend."

Laura Doyle, another of Missy's friends, also seemed to have trouble accepting the fact that she was never going to see her schoolmate and neighbour again. She broke down in tears at the funeral and sent Irene a touching sympathy card. "It said that she was heartbroken about what happened to my daughter. That not only was I Missy's mother but hers too.

"She came over to my house all depressed. She said she wanted to commit suicide because she was the last person to see Missy alive.

"Laura had picked Missy up the afternoon she died. They were laughing and joking. My daughter ran out in a real good mood. Her last words were: 'We're going to the park. I'll call you at eight.' At 6pm Laura called and asked to speak to Missy. I said, 'What are you talking about? She's with you.' She said, 'No, I left her at the park.' "

Irene waited up all night for Missy. "At two in the morning, I thought to myself, 'Boy, is she going to get it.' But I was scared. I knew something had happened to her. I just knew it."

The next morning a distraught Irene called the cops in Arleta, a suburb of Los Angeles in the San Fernando Valley, and a search was launched. Laura told police she'd dropped Missy off at a park while she put petrol in her car. But as she drove off, she noticed Missy talking to two young men in a blue Chevrolet Camaro. When she came back they were gone.

Two days later, hikers found her body in a picturesque creek running through a forested area of Big Tajunga Canyon in Angeles National Forest. Missy's lovely, long brown hair had been chopped off in clumps and her head had been held under six inches of water until she'd drowned. Her killer, or killers, had placed a large log on top of her body in a feeble attempt to hide it.

Recalling the bitter day she learned the tragic news, Irene

said: "It was like a bad dream, and I kept hoping I'd wake up.

"It was really rough at Christmas because I'd go shopping and I'd see the back of a girl that looked like her. And I'd think, 'Oh my God'. "

Irene, who has three grown sons, was not just traumatised by her daughter's death, she was also upset that she didn't know who'd killed her. But she could always turn for support to both Karen and Laura, who were willing to rush over if she needed anything or just someone to talk to.

Karen often told Irene that she wanted to avenge Missy's death. "She'd always tell me, 'The minute we find the animal who did this I will be sitting right next to you in the courtroom.' "

Frustrated by the homicide squad's failure to find suspects in the case, Irene carried out her own manhunt for drivers of blue Camaros.

She said: "I would stop guys in the street at 11 at night and make them get out of their cars. Karen would be right next to me the whole time. I harassed innocent guys."

Karen and Laura helped out with Irene's murder hunt, even going down to the police station for her to get the latest information on the case. Karen also gave Irene the names of Missy's boyfriends who may have had a reason to kill her. But the leads came to nothing.

For three years, the heartbroken mum went to bed each night praying that police would catch the killers. But when cops did finally make an arrest, the identity of the suspects was more than she could bear.

"It was like someone punched me in the stomach. I was shocked. I walked to my room and passed out."

Karen Severson and Laura Doyle were charged with killing Missy in a jealous rage because she'd slept with their boyfriends.

"Now I know why Karen was here so much," says Irene. "She wanted to be one step ahead of everyone else. She and Laura made fools out of all of us. And I trusted Karen so much. We all trusted her. She was my daughter's best friend. They grew up together. That girl was part of this family.''

The deadly duo would have got off scot-free except for a guilt-ridden friend of Missy's who was with the girls that fateful October day. Eva Chirumbolo, now 23, had been haunted by the murder, but told police she was too frightened of the killers to come forward earlier.

"I was afraid for myself, that my life would be in danger,'' she said, adding that Laura and Karen warned her they would blame her for the murder. Eva decided to speak up after her 18-year-old brother's suicide made her realise the grief Irene and her sons were feeling.

At the trial, Eva testified that after Karen had picked her up, they met Missy and Laura. Then they drove in both cars to their canyon hideaway, where they often went to drink beer and smoke pot. Eva told the court Karen said she was going to "scare" Missy. And when they arrived at the creek, Karen and Laura began taunting Missy about all the boys she'd been to bed with, including their boyfriends.

At one point, Laura grabbed Missy by the hair and accused her of having slept with Victor Amaya, Laura's boyfriend. While still sitting in the car, Missy was crying when Laura suddenly grabbed her by the wrist and said: "Let's go for a walk.''

The four of them walked down to the creek. Laura then stepped into the water and Karen pushed Missy towards her. Laura grabbed Missy by the wrist again and pulled her into the water.

Eva was so scared things were getting out of control that she ran back to her car. She said: "Then I heard a scream — so loud. I just froze. I could not go back down that hill. I just sat there between the cars and just waited.''

Minutes later the other girls joined her — without Missy. Karen quickly drove off, leaving Eva to go home with Laura. "She was laughing and crying," said Eva, "and she was saying, 'Ha, ha, ha. We killed Missy'. ''

Laura said Missy deserved to die because she had slept

with her boyfriend Victor. Asked why she didn't stop the fight, Eva replied: "I don't know. I just didn't know how far it was going to go."

But Laura's lawyer Charles Lloyd claimed that Chirumbolo only came forward after rumours began to spread linking her to the murder. He also pointed out that Eva's boyfriend John Avril had a crush on Missy and the girls had had a bitchy row only weeks before the murder. "It's obscene that Chirumbolo is not charged with this killing," said Lloyd.

Severson's attorney Harold Vites said: "If Karen and Laura had this elaborate plan to kill Missy, why would they take Eva along if she was not part of the plan? That doesn't make a whole lot of sense."

But Deputy District Attorney Tamia Hope said: "Eva is not an accomplice to this crime. If she was really involved, why didn't she just keep quiet?"

Victor Amaya, 23, swayed the jury, however, when he testified that Laura had threatened to kill Missy six weeks before the murder. Then Irene revealed that Karen had visited her house to talk about a problem with Missy. "She started to tell me a bunch of dirty things about my daughter. She said Missy took everybody's boyfriends and that she was a big flirt. I just told her: 'If you're not going to talk properly, just get out.' "

Irene also recalled that Missy and Karen often had big rows "over boys" and at the time of her death they had not been talking for a month. "They had an argument over this guy Karen was living with, Randy Fernandez. My daughter used to go out with him first."

Severson and Doyle, who were tried as adults although only 17 at the time of the crime, were charged with first-degree murder. But the jury was not convinced the killing had been planned and had trouble believing Eva's testimony. Instead they convicted both of them of second-degree murder.

One juror said: "There just wasn't any proof that it was

premeditated. We thought they got carried away and didn't know when to stop. And Eva was probably holding something back to protect herself.''

Severson and Doyle, now both 24, were sentenced in 1990 to at least 15 years in jail, but will be eligible for parole in 1997. Both women have appealed.

Freelance reporter Karen Kingsbury has written a book about the case, which is now being turned into a TV movie.

Irene, meanwhile, says she'll never recover from her daughter's murder. ''My life has been shattered forever because of this cold-blooded and senseless act. They cut off Missy's hair to make her look ugly. That was their way of torturing her. And they left her to die in the woods like an animal. I keep thinking that Missy will finally be able to rest in peace. But for me, it will never be over. You can't get over losing a child. That just doesn't happen. When they killed her, they killed a part of me.''

13

The Perfect Teacher?

John Garris was perfect for the teaching job. He was bright, well-dressed, and spoke eloquently. His references were impeccable and he had two college degrees. But, deep down, he was keeping a dark secret from thousands of schoolchildren – he was a convicted killer on the run from the law after escaping from prison.

The education department of Fairfax County, on the outskirts of Washington, DC had desperately needed good teachers and Garris fitted the bill to a T. Garris, 38, was offered a position as a substitute teacher, and had an excellent chance of getting a full-time post.

Although he specialised in maths and science, he was asked to teach a variety of subjects at a dozen secondary schools because he had a vast all-round knowledge. He soon took up a regular position at Whitman Intermediate School, where he turned up every day in smart suits and expensive ties.

The headmaster, Garris's colleagues and especially the kids all gave him top marks. That was, until the FBI came to the school one afternoon and arrested him.

Hundreds of students and teachers watched from classroom windows as Garris was led away in handcuffs. The gossip soon spread through the school corridors that he was a fugitive killer.

"The children were never in any danger," says Garris, who once hit a jail guard on the head. "At no time did I bring them any harm."

And Whitman's headmaster Eugene Jordan said: "Kids were very upset about the fact that he's not going to be a substitute here any more."

After a few minor offences as a teenager, Garris was sentenced in 1974 to 45 years for brutally beating, robbing and strangling a 71-year-old man.

"I got involved with a couple of bad guys I hardly knew," he maintains. "I was only 20 at the time. We got involved in a minor robbery that escalated into a murder."

In June 1991, Garris escaped from a car that was taking him back from his work-release programme at Rosewood State Hospital to the Maryland House of Correction in Jessup, near Baltimore.

He said: "Because I'd been in jail for so long, the only thing I'd learned was that when you get a chance to escape you go for it. I had a propensity for negative behaviour."

Prisoners on work-release programmes are allowed to carry £30 in their pocket and Garris used the money to track down friends who helped to hide him. While working on various jobs as a labourer, he kept moving between three different flats – one in Virginia, another in Washington and the other in Maryland.

He also found himself a girlfriend. "She was a mother of two kids, and the first time we had sex it was unbelievable. I hadn't made love for 18 years."

After his arrest, Garris shocked FBI men by claiming that during his year as a fugitive he worked in the White House. He told them that "influential friends" on Capitol Hill got him a job, with full security clearance, painting President Bush's basement for two weeks.

Garris said he had a great time helping the kids at Whitman get an education so they wouldn't end up in jail like him.

"They looked up to me. I gave them things I always wanted to hear as a kid. They need people like me who really care. I took a job as a teacher so I could do something worthwhile while I was out. It was my responsibility to help them understand the subject matter. Most of them weren't very up on their lessons.

"My students often said they liked me, that I was teaching

them the way it was supposed to be done. They were so impressed with my methods that they often told me about problems in their personal lives to see if I could help out there as well. One of the things that I would do was let them know that they were much better people than they often thought they were, and better than what other people said about them. I remember in one class students were passing around a piece of paper. I confiscated it. But it was a petition to the principal, demanding that he permanently assign me to the school. I gave the petition back to the kids and they handed it to the principal. I was waiting to find out whether I was going to get a full-time job when I was arrested.

"I later confiscated another piece of paper on which the kids said things like they loved me and they thought I was the best teacher. I was so badly treated as a kid that I wanted these children to be the best that they could be. Not only did I teach them the subject, I taught them things about life. I often acted as a counsellor and we developed a close and trusting relationship. I treated them all equally and loved them so much. I really miss them."

On his job application, Garris said he'd never been convicted of any offence, which he admits now was a blatant lie.

But he also claimed he'd received a Bachelor of Science degree in applied psychology from Coppin State College, where he said he graduated in 1978. He did, in fact, have a degree from the college but he never attended the graduation ceremonies.

Garris was behind bars at the time and got his degree through a correspondence course. He also passed another degree in human services through the mail. He even taught other prisoners.

Fairfax County education supervisor Alan Leis said that Garris's personal references, which included a letter from Senator Charles Robb's office, were genuine and contained "very high marks and very good comments".

But Leis didn't bother to look into them or his college

education because he thought there was nothing more he could learn about Garris by double-checking. A simple phone call, of course, would have revealed that Garris got his degree while doing his homework in jail.

"He was interested in working and he was anxious to work so we called him often," said Leis. "Who would think an escaped convicted murderer would apply for a substitute teaching job?"

But Garris was tired of doing various exhausting blue-collar jobs and aspired to be a white-collar worker. So he wrote in for a job as a substitute even though it only paid £30 a day.

"When I applied, I never tried to hide anything. I wanted them to know I was who I said I was." And up to a point that was true. He gave his real name and correct address. If county officials had bothered to check on his address, they would have found it was a shelter for homeless men which he stayed at now and then.

To become a substitute, Garris had to have his fingerprints taken and he freely obliged. Schools in Virginia have required fingerprinting since 1988 when a school psychologist was arrested for molesting children.

At the time Garris applied, Fairfax County officials did not wait for the results of fingerprint checks before teachers started work.

It takes up to 10 weeks to get them back and there is such a huge turnover of teachers that there could be a staffing shortage.

But Garris was certain his prints would not show up on Virginia's criminal files. He'd got a job working at the White House part-time without any trouble and thought it would be easier to pass security checks for a teaching job.

However, he did not realise that his fingerprints were then passed on to the FBI to see if he had served time or was a fugitive from elsewhere in the nation.

About 30 applicants a year are found to have criminal records. Two months after Garris had started working, the

FBI discovered he was a wanted man. When he had escaped, Garris had only a few months left to serve in jail before he was paroled.

He told the FBI that he ran off because he'd been falsely accused of sexually abusing a mentally disturbed man at Rosewood State Hospital, where he was working as a counsellor. Garris, who has spent more than half his life behind bars, is now facing another 10 years in jail — which could be added on to his murder sentence.

Fairfax County, which needs 93,000 substitutes a year, has now changed its teacher hiring policy. It now refuses to let teachers start work until their prints have been cleared by the FBI.

Garris, meanwhile, is looking forward to the day when he finally gets out of jail: "I know what I want to be now — a teacher."

14

Marianne Alexander

The peeping Tom crept down the dark hallway into sultry student Marianne Alexander's bedroom. He pulled back the blankets, slowly lifted her nightgown and pulled down her knickers to her knees. But she suddenly woke up and screamed in terror. To silence her, he hammered poor Marianne over the head repeatedly with a heavy object.

That was the blood-curdling beginning to a 10-year murder mystery that terrorised a university campus and a small American town. It was only after a crack cop handled the chilling case as a last resort that students and local residents could go to sleep at night feeling safe in their beds – without being afraid that the sick killer would strike again.

The 22-year-old brunette was found four hours later, still breathing, by her roommate Susan Hoyt, who'd left the front door unlocked when she went out earlier that night. She thought her friend was making strange noises so she turned on the light to see what was wrong, and to her horror she saw Marianne's face was covered in blood and there was blood on the curtains and the ceiling.

The nursing student at Lowell University in Massachusetts died of massive brain damage the next day, with her parents and her two sisters by her side. "She never regained consciousness," said her father David, a retired design engineer for General Electric. "The doctors gave us no hope – all we could do was hold her hand until she died. Marianne was a wonderful child. We never had a moment's trouble with her. She was such a happy kid. She was a quiet, straight-A student and had never had a date in her life. She would have made a great nurse.''

Police were baffled by the gruesome murder on that freezing February night in 1980. The possibility that Marianne had had a row with her three flatmates was ruled out after Susan took a lie-detector test along with students Catherine LeBourdais and Eileen Maloney, who had both been away on a skiing trip. A robbery motive was dismissed because nothing was taken, but a rape attempt was likely because her clothing had been tampered with. Police chief Len Macphail said at the time: ''Whoever killed Marianne knew the victim and her flatmates or knew that four young women were living in the apartment.'' But that's all they had to go on − except for a ''suspicious-looking person'' who was seen by Hoyt in the vicinity that night carrying an unidentified object. He turned out to be a neighbour and was immediately dubbed the ''prime suspect'' by the cops. But his alibi that he was buying stereo equipment at the time of the murder was soon confirmed by witnesses.

Police quizzed several boyfriends of Marianne's flatmates, but came up with no new clues to the callous killer. And despite searching a mountain of garbage at a landfill with a metal detector, cops were unable to find the murder weapon, at first believed to be a hammer.

The investigation dragged on for years until eventually the massive file was stored with other cases of unsolved murders in the tiny mill town of 130,000 people. Frightened students at Lowell kept their doors firmly locked, while nervous neighbours like Louise Podanoffsky lived in fear of the murderer in their midst. She said: ''We never knew if he'd come back one day and do it again.'' And Marianne's heartbroken mother Harriet said: ''I never thought I'd learn what really happened to my daughter − who killed her and why.''

Then a new police chief dusted off the file and handed it to top cop David Tousignant, who was named Lowell Officer of the Year in 1988. He spent four months poring over reports and at first he was puzzled, too. "There was no clear cut reason why this girl should die," he said. "None of the normal scenarios in a murder were present."

His investigation took him full circle — back to the original prime suspect, bizarre bachelor Roland Douglas Phinney. The detective discovered that Phinney was a troubled loner with a kinky fascination for taking semi-pornographic photos of young women, mostly without their knowledge by zoom lens. The 47-year-old technician, a small bespectacled man who'd been a lifelong member of the local baptist church choir, had lived almost his entire life with his parents right next door to the murder house.

Tousignant first came across his name when he began questioning Marianne's flatmates again. One recalled that two weeks before the murder a pair of panties had disappeared from her room. Phinney's mother Doris had returned them, saying her son found them after they'd blown over the fence while they were being hung out to dry. But none of the girls had ever hung clothes out on the line. Next the officer learned that Phinney was known as the local peeping Tom because he was often spotted by neighbours sneaking into backyards to grab photos of women sunbathing.

The obsessive cop also noticed that the one letter of sympathy that the Alexander family had received from a stranger was written by Phinney's mother. Then a friend of Phinney's, Josep Amaral, revealed that during a conversation about the murder Phinney muttered something about "proof" — adding that the cops "ain't so smart".

Amaral said: "Phinney loved pornographic videos, particularly ones that depicted women in bondage. He had a very negative attitude towards women, never rated them and often referred to them in a vulgar manner." Another friend of Phinney's, Roland Bartell, said: "He would rant on and on about the girls living next door to him, what a good view he had of the girls from his upstairs window."

Amaral, 72, also told police that Phinney had a favourite

hand-held camera flash that he used constantly before the murder, but two days after the brutal beating he noticed that it was dented. He asked Phinney about it and the voyeur amateur photographer replied that he'd smashed it in a fit of anger when it wouldn't work. Tousignant said: "I began looking at old metal flashes and realised they were similar to a hammer. I took a facsimile one to the pathologist and asked him if it could be the weapon and he said yes." Then when he checked on Phinney's alibi, he learned that it was not as airtight as he first believed. Phinney had been at the stereo store much earlier than he'd previously claimed.

Phinney also appeared to be a perfect match to a profile of the killer drawn up eight years earlier by the FBI. It said that the killer would live close to the crime scene, only had a high-school degree and had never been arrested. The profile also said that the killer probably engaged in peeping Tom activities and the theft of ladies' underwear. He would be a quiet person who had difficulty dealing with members of the opposite sex.

Tousignant believed he now had enough to bring Phinney in for questioning. While the suspect was still at the police station, Tousignant went to his home armed with a search warrant. In his room, the police found a collection of pornographic video tapes and nearly 10,000 photos of women. Some were dressed in swimsuits, some in mini-skirts, and some were naked; while other photos consisted of close-ups of breasts, buttocks, legs and vaginas. He'd destroyed photos of Marianne and her flatmates but there were pictures of other women who'd lived in the house that were taken while they were sunbathing in bikinis in the back garden. Incredibly, the police also found the murder weapon – the Yushika flash, which was badly bent out of shape. "He could not bear to throw it away – or maybe he wanted to hold on to it as some type of trophy," said Tousignant.

When he was told the Yushika flash was intact, the dogged detective stepped up the questioning and finally after nine years of silence Phinney cracked under the strain, admitting he'd killed Marianne after she woke up while he was trying to take a nude picture of her. He said that after he'd looked through Marianne's window and saw she was asleep, he entered the unlocked apartment and made his way down a dark corridor to her room. In his hand-written, four-page confession, he continued: "I had just gotten her underwear down when she woke and saw me. I could see she was frightened. I grabbed the camera and started hitting her with it. I saw her bleeding from the head so I took off." He ran home and threw away his blood-stained clothes.

Phinney told Tousignant that he did not have to kill her but he panicked because he was afraid of what his domineering mother would do if she found out. She had already threatened to kick him out of the house if she found him watching pornographic videos or stealing panties again. In the end, Tousignant almost felt sorry for him. "He was a loner whose world revolved around his camera and photographs. That was his way of interacting with women. It was the closest he felt he could get to them."

Phinney claimed at his trial that he made up the confession following hours of gruelling interrogation. "I figured the police weren't going to let me go until I said something." But he was found guilty and was sentenced recently to life in prison without parole.

Marianne's mother was delighted with the verdict, saying: "Her soul will finally be at rest now. And so will mine, knowing that her killer is behind bars forever. We can now get on with our lives and finally put this thing to rest."

15

Poetic Justice

If David Schoenecker's plans had succeeded, 55 people would be dead. But after the first murder he left a giveaway clue to be read.

He wanted to enjoy the last laugh by leaving an amusing little poem near his wife's corpse. And then David Schoenecker, 50, intended to go rampaging on the orgy of violence he'd planned. But it was Judge Robert Fitzgerald who laughed the longest, after sentencing the killer with a short ditty of his own.

Schoenecker, a chemical engineer from Anaheim Hills, California, had drawn up a 'hit list' of 54 relatives and former friends he had grudges against, including his first wife. Many of these were from Milwaukee, Wisconsin, where he used to live. He had tried to explain his feelings to his second wife, Gail, but she was horrified by the thoughts going round in his head. Schoenecker decided he had to do away with her before she gave his vicious plan away.

His evil scheme began with a romantic, candlelit dinner on 5 May, 1989. After it, Gail, a 40-year-old schoolteacher, fell asleep. Then the voluntary Sunday school teacher shot his wife in the head with a .357 Magnum.

Afterwards, Schoenecker left his sick little rhyme on a table in clear view, for the police to find. The verse he had written was a perversion of the well-known Christmas song, *Santa Claus Is Coming to Town.*

"I made my list, I'm checking it twice. I'm going to find out who's naughty, not nice. All I seek is real revenge. And I want it made very clear they have taken from me things

80

that I've held very dear. This plan has taken three years to prepare. I've hidden weapons and money everywhere. I'll come in the night, I'll come in the day. I've chosen for each their own special way. All on the list will go to their grave, all with the help of friendly old Dave.''

Armed with his copy of the hit list, his Magnum and $4,000 in savings, Schoenecker headed for Montana, where his next victim lived.

However, Schoenecker could not resist bragging about his plan and his poem. So he wrote to his favourite columnist on the local paper − Bob Emmers of the *Orange County Register*. A chilling excerpt from Schoenecker's rambling letter, which also gave details of his hit list, reads:

''Last Friday I killed my wife. There is a very strong possibility that no one has discovered her body so I suggest you have the police check 7871 East Amanda Circle. There was no hatred. I loved her − but the action was necessary because I have a purpose − one that cannot have any interference. Over the past few years I have had images that I know what is going to happen before it occurs.

''At first I simply dismissed these sensations, but when I started to see certain events very clearly, I knew there was more to this than just daydreams or nightmares. What I was seeing were events in my life involving people that had done wrong or evil against me. The feeling is that all will be made right and I will be the force to make it right.''

The paper contacted the police, who broke into Schoenecker's house and found his wife's rotting body. She had been dead for five days.

When the police notified potential victims, some on the list said that they'd never heard of Schoenecker.

David Nuss, who appeared on the hit list and had played with Schoenecker on the school football team, said: ''I didn't sleep well until they captured him.'' And Schoenecker's ex-wife Kathy, to whom he was married for 15 years, recalled, ''I was scared to death. I panicked.'' But she couldn't remember him ever being violent.

Right: David Schoenecker brutally murdered his second wife, Gail.

Below: David Schoenecker (right) in court with his attourney.

"He loved to be in control and I didn't want anyone running my life. I guess the other people on the list felt the same way as me."

Her daughter Traci, 22, added: "I can't believe that my own father has killed my stepmom and wanted to murder my mother. I was petrified."

Schoenecker admitted later that it might have been a "bit foolish" to send a letter to the paper saying where he was going, but he thought he would have plenty of time to escape. Except a flat tyre let him down — and once he had abandoned his car and started hiking towards the scenic Hoodoo pass, across the 7,000-foot snow-capped peaks of the Bitterroot forest mountain range, on his way to Idaho, it was only a matter of time before he was caught.

Schoenecker claimed he'd suffered temporary insanity when he killed his wife and wrote the bizarre poem. But Sheriff Chet Barry said: "He didn't suddenly snap. It was all thought out over at least three years."

The final nail in Schoenecker's coffin was the evidence that he had cancelled all postal deliveries a day before the killing. "He wasn't going to be there and he planned that she wasn't going to be there either," said prosecutor Chris Evans. In August 1989, a jury found David Schoenecker guilty of murder in the first degree. When he was sentenced two months later, Judge Robert Fitzgerald recited his own little rhyme.

"You won't kill in the night, nor kill in the day. All on your list can go on their merry way. You killed your sweet wife who loved you so dear. For that you're being punished, let me make that fact clear. The sentence I've chosen to you may seem cold. You'll pay, and you'll pay all the while you'll grow old. One day you will die, a funeral your warden will hold. For you will serve your entire natural life and not be paroled."

Although Fitzgerald has been criticised in some quarters for his frivolous delivery, many feel his sentence has ensured more than poetic justice. Schoenecker will end his days in Chino State Jail.

16

How Many Did One Single Shot Kill?

The callous murder of petrol-station hand William "Petey" Norwood wasted a young life. But when his mother carried out his last wish, for his body to be used to help others, she set off a chain reaction of fear and death all over America. For, unbeknown to her, Petey had the deadly AIDS virus. Over six years later, how he caught it is still a mystery. And his killer stays free.

Quiet, carefree 22-year-old Petey Norwood gave his mum a shock when he disclosed a premonition — that he'd die young. How could he have known that a week later he'd be shot dead by a bandit during a robbery that went tragically wrong? Or did he know something about his health that he never revealed to a soul . . . that he had AIDS?

A single shot from a robber's gun killed William Norwood. But that one murder is now being blamed for death after death. Because Petey left all his organs for transplants. Each of them carrying the HIV virus.

Norwood was working nights at a petrol station in the Virginia farming town of Dinwiddie when the robber aimed a gun at him and demanded money. Petey wasn't quick enough. So the bandit shot him in the head, grabbed $100 from the till and fled.

The dying man was taken to Petersburg General Hospital — now renamed the Southside Regional Medical Center. There, after a vain 12-hour fight to save him, his mother, Bessie Rathbone, gave permission for all his organs to be used for transplants. Only a week earlier, in August 1985, he'd told his mum to donate his organs when he died.

Before any organs were taken, Norwood's body was given

routine tests for AIDS. He was found to be "clean". Not that anyone would have suspected him of carrying the HIV virus, as he wasn't known to be in any of the high-risk categories: homosexual, drug user, or a haemophiliac needing blood transfusions.

All usable organs were taken out and fresh-frozen like peas. Sterilising them first might have spoiled the organs. Not sterilising them left the unsuspected AIDS virus very much alive.

The organs were soon requested by a non-profit organisation called LifeNet and shipped off within hours to 30 hospitals all over the United States. Hospitals where desperate patients waited for the chance of a life-saving transplant. Bessie Rathbone might have lost a well-loved son. But at least, she thought, she'd done her bit for others. She could not have been more wrong.

In 1986, the man who was given Norwood's heart died of AIDS. Two years later, the patient given one of his kidneys also died of AIDS. In 1990, the man who got Norwood's other kidney went the same way. The patient who received the liver died of "complications after surgery". The one who was given the pancreas has never been traced.

The scandal erupted when an elderly woman in Colorado, who'd been given one of Norwood's hip joints, tested positive for HIV four years ago. Health officials first thought she had caught the AIDS virus from a blood transfusion. But when they checked they found her bone graft had been done without a transfusion.

Despite this discovery, Colorado's state medical authorities did not warn LifeNet, who handle around 30,000 human organ donations every year.

And it was not until last year that the alarm went out. LifeNet tested cells preserved from the murdered man. And discovered he had AIDS. Hospital officials all over America began searching for 50 more people who had been given various kinds of tissue from Norwood's body. Tissue grafts including bone, tendons, ligaments and skin are used for

The scene of the murder.
Inset: William 'Petey' Norwood.

a wide range of surgical procedures such as dentistry, cancer surgery and dealing with athletic injuries. So far, three people given grafts from Norwood have caught the AIDS virus.

People who got skin or bone grafts may be luckier than others. Skin and bone tissue is exposed to radiation, or treated with Ethyl alcohol, to kill off germs before being freeze-dried. But the safeguard is not foolproof.

"We can't be 100 per cent certain that it kills the AIDS virus," says a Food and Drug Administration official. "But it does reduce the risk."

Norwood's bone marrow had been sent to the US Navy – but it was recovered before any of it had been used. Two people given the corneas from his eyes were also lucky: tests showed they didn't have AIDS. And tests on a handful of other potential victims have also proved negative.

"This case is tragic, unfortunate," says LifeNet official Doug Wilson. "But we were not at all negligent. The science simply was not there in 1985. And the likelihood of this happening today is slim-to-zero."

Petey's auntie, Emma Norwood, who is Bessie Rathbone's sister, says: "It made us feel so much better arranging for transplants. After Petey died, my sister and I said, 'What we'd love to know is who got his heart – because that would make us feel he was still alive.' All we wanted was to help somebody else out."

The sisters were upset to find out how many of Petey's organs had been taken for medical use. "It was bad enough that he was murdered," Emma says. "But all this AIDS thing has brought it back. It's like Petey died all over again.

"And Bessie was mad as hell, because she thought the doctors were saying they would only remove her son's heart, kidneys and spine, and then she heard about all those other things that were taken and sent all over the United States."

LifeNet's president Dr Richard Hurwitz has called for all state health departments to report on transplant-AIDS cases immediately, in future. But the baffling, vital question still remains: how did Petey Norwood catch AIDS in the first place?

Friends and relatives all remember him as a carefree, normal young man who loved to go out boozing, fix up cars and cruise the back roads in his blue Ford Ranchero wagon. He was no stranger to trouble, they admit. But, they insist, definitely not gay. And not into hard drugs and needles.

Petey's petrol-station colleague, Steve Shifflett, says "It was a real shock when I heard he had AIDS."

And Walter Reese, who managed another petrol station not far from Petey's, declares: "He was ordinary enough, seemed happy-go-lucky. He and my stepson went out drinking and to the bowling alley, just like other kids that age. My wife, Pat, was so upset when he was shot, that she set up a reward for catching the killer."

Despite Petey's legion of loyal supporters, some people in the community have been wondering whether he was a secret homosexual, or had a hidden drug problem. But his best friend, Chip Wright, is outraged by such rumours. "It's a smear campaign," he says. "Nobody even wonders whether it might have happened in the hospital."

One unnamed woman friend said, "I miss Petey a lot. He always made me laugh."

Waitress Mary Harlan, who worked across the street from Petey's Exxon station, says, "The only way I can figure it is that Petey caught AIDS in hospital, from transfusions when they were trying to save him."

But some health officials wonder if the hospital tests of 1985 — far less sophisticated than today's — just failed to pick up the virus. Dr Harold Jaffee, AIDS department director at the government's Centre for Disease Control, says: "Norwood probably got the virus just before he was shot. So it didn't show in tests.

"If you're going to use organs for transplants, there's a small chance you're going to miss someone who's been infected so soon before death that he has not yet produced antibodies against HIV.

"Routine AIDS tests register only the antibodies, not the virus itself. So there is this 'window' of infection that can last between four weeks and a year, without being traced."

Virginia Health Department chief Dr Martin Cader says: "We're investigating the possibility that Mr Norwood was infected by a transfusion. But it's a remote chance, because the tests run on blood donors are very reliable — if not 100 per cent."

Among those for whom that chance could mean life or death are four cops under Dinwiddie Sheriff Benny Heath, who heads the murder hunt. They carried the dying man from the petrol station and fear his blood may have given them the deadly virus.

These days Petey's mum is still outraged that her boy's killer has never been arrested, despite a $5,000 reward put up by his employers.

"The police are not interested in catching the person who murdered my son," Bessie Rathbone claims. "They are only interested in him because of the AIDS. Yet before he got shot he was never sick.

"They've told me over and over again that they know who the killer is, but don't have enough evidence to charge him with murder.

"I call the sheriff's office every now and again and give 'em hell. Because whoever is walking round out there has got off scot-free."

17

The Three Wives of Dr Strangelove

Norman Lewiston had a lot on his plate. The 52-year-old
doctor had three wives to keep happy. In an extraordinary
juggling act, Lewiston kept secret from the three women —
who incidentally knew each other — the fact that he was
married to all of them at once.

And as Norman flitted from one wife to another, his
weight ballooned to over 17 stone and pushed him to an early
grave. Not surprising — since he often ended up eating two
or three big dinners in an evening just to keep the three Mrs
Lewistons happy.

Wife No 3, Robyn Lewiston, 42, said; "I know for a fact
that he had three turkey dinners one Thanksgiving Day."
And wife No 2, Katy Lewiston, 44, said, "Norman was so
overweight, he was eating all the meals three wives were
feeding him."

His first wife, Diana Lewiston, 51, recalls they had lunch
"every Friday" — the same day Katy swears he regularly
had lunch with her.

Incredibly, Norman juggled his wives while holding down
a stressful job as a professor of paediatrics at the Stanford
Children's Hospital, in Palo Alto, northern California. He
also headed a cystic fibrosis clinic and helped to develop the
first heart-lung transplant programme for child sufferers of
the deadly disease. But, despite his six-figure salary, he owed
£40,000 on his credit cards after trying to support three
homes. Norman was paying the mortgage on two houses,
rent on a small flat plus his three kids' college tuition fees.

On 5 August, 1991, Norman had dinner with Katy before
dashing off to the hospital, where he supposedly often stayed

the night. Katy let him sleep there because "He snored so loudly that I couldn't sleep. I let him come to bed with me whenever he wanted but he slept at the hospital."

That night, as usual, he drove to Diana's house. While in bed with her Norman died of a heart attack brought on by high blood pressure. Katy got the terrible news the next day from the hospital. "In one call, I learned my husband was dead and the woman who brought him in was also married to him."

She got an even bigger shock when she went to Norman's office. Katy found photos of her husband with Diana and Robyn. She recognised Robyn immediately as they had both worked with the bearded doctor. Katy found Robyn's number and called, suspecting the worst. Robyn told her: "Norm and I married two years ago. He said he'd divorced you."

Says Katy, "It was awful — I lost 12lbs in seven days, I couldn't eat or sleep. I loved him so much and thought he was an extremely loyal man. But it's turned into a nightmare. It hurt, not just the financial problems, but the betrayal, too."

Robyn added, "I believe he loved all three of us, but was incapable of letting any of us go. Once you had a relationship with Norm, you had it for life. And there was a strong sexual attraction. Just because people don't spend the night together doesn't mean they don't have sex."

Although the unmerry widows say they still love him, they also hate Norman for the lies he told over the years. It all began when Norman walked down the aisle with Diana when he was 21.

They had three children — David, 27, James, 24, and Pamela, 20. But by the '70s he was cheating on his wife, usually with women from the hospital. Robyn was a nurse, Katy an administrator.

At a Christmas party, Robyn was one of several women who queued up as a joke to kiss Dr Lewiston. He declared Robyn the winner. Within days they were dating each other.

Norman showered her with gifts and took her to Europe on holiday. She even met his mum. Diana found out about the affair but accepted that she and Norman were leading separate lives. She even called Robyn and said, "As long as he does not divorce me, he can do anything."

Five years later, Robyn gave Norman an ultimatum – divorce Diana and marry me or it's over. He showed her divorce papers but she had them checked and was told they were forged. So Robyn moved 800 miles away to San Diego. Later Norman moved in, claiming he'd quit his job and planned to marry her.

The next six months were the happiest of Robyn's life. But then Norman told her he'd only taken a sabbatical from work. "It was obvious he'd gone back to his job and also Diana. That was very hurtful," said Robyn.

Although Norman was back with Diana, he was up to his old tricks. He bumped into Katy and asked her out. "I thought he'd divorced Diana as I knew he'd been living with Robyn."

Norman and Katy got engaged but, says Katy, "When I mentioned the wedding, he'd change the subject." She stepped up the pressure after they bought a house in Los Altos, just 10 miles from Diana's home. Her dream came true on 6 November, 1985, when they were married. But the wedding night was a disappointment. "Norman left for the hospital to work while I painted our living room for the reception."

Katy became his public wife who attended office functions and parties. Even when they bumped into Diana, who was giving demonstrations in a shopping mall, he brazened out the introductions. Katy thought she was meeting his ex; Diana always turned a blind eye to his other women.

Meanwhile, Robyn had married a dentist and had a daughter. But they split up after two years together. Norman had kept in contact with her and wrote: "Katy and I are growing distant. It won't be long before one of us gets itchy feet."

After Robyn's divorce, Norman began flying to San Diego

at weekends, telling his two wives he was doing research there. Robyn says, "I assumed he'd divorced Diana because he'd married Katy. And when he told me he'd divorced Katy, I believed him as they were together such a short time."

In September 1989, Norman and Robyn were married. The devious doctor told his bride that he had to continue living up north for two more years so he'd be eligible for his pension. Robyn believed he was sleeping at the hospital every night. He even rented a room near the hospital — conveniently situated between Diana's and Katy's homes — so they could be together when Robyn visited.

Says Katy: "I never once thought he was cheating on me. He didn't call me Robyn or Diana or use general names like darling."

But eventually the dirty doc's luck ran out. Robyn came north to a hospital do. Norman introduced her to a colleague, who said, "I met you at a party a while back." Robyn replied, "I haven't been to one with Norm."

He said the colleague had mixed up her dates. But Robyn searched his briefcase and found a letter addressed to him at Katy's house. "I knew deep down I had to say goodbye. It's hard to admit there are some marriages you walk away from."

She called in a private eye, who found out Norman was a bigamist. Robyn's lawyer demanded £10,000 to settle the marriage and she got a cheque in three days.

Six weeks later, Norman died before signing the annulment papers. Diana, the sole beneficiary in his will and executor of his estate, is suing Katy for half her house. Katy is suing his estate for fraud, in an attempt to hold on to the house and get a share of his pension.

Robyn jokes, "The only thing I want to inherit are his frequent flyer air miles." The revelations about his tangled love life led to an investigation of a research fund he handled. Auditors suspect he used £5,000 of it to settle debts.

The three wives have been considering offers of

Hollywood movie rights to the Lewiston story. And Katy is writing a book about him.

"It's easy to fantasise about the fun Norm had but I think it was hell for him," said a colleague. "He was in a complete mess and didn't have the character to get himself out of it."

18

Please! I Didn't Kill My Baby

To see your tiny baby fall sick and die is horror enough. But for Patti Stallings, that tragedy turned into the nightmare of a murder charge. Only the sadness of a second sickly child saved her from a lifetime spent behind bars.

Patti Stallings cuddles her son David, two, distraught that he was born with a dangerous illness. Yet she also knows it was only the discovery of that illness which proved her innocent of murdering his brother.

For Patti, now 26, and her husband Dave, the nightmare began on 7 July, 1989. Their first-born, three-month-old Ryan, had never been able to keep his bottle-feed down. And suddenly, that morning, he lay obviously in pain in his cot, breathing unnaturally.

Patti rushed Ryan to hospital. After three days of tests on him, his parents were taken to the local police station in St Louis, Missouri.

The tests had shown ethylene glycol — used in anti-freeze — in the child's blood. And the police suspected the parents of poisoning him. Detectives grilled Patti and Dave separately. Patti was asked if she'd suffered post-natal depression or been jealous of the attention her husband paid to the baby?

Dave was asked if they'd been fighting a lot — and if he, rather than Patti, had been jealous of the baby. They told him his wife had failed a lie-detector test. That, itself, was a big lie. He nearly fell for it. "But," he says now, "my senses came back and I thought, 'They're crazy!'"

After 12 days in hospital, baby Ryan recovered. But he was put into foster care. The heartbroken parents were only

95

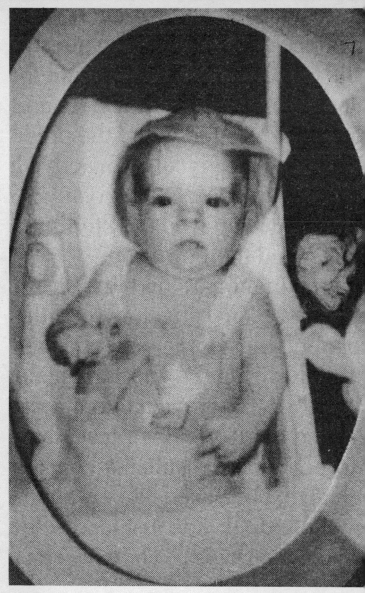

The death of Ryan meant a double horror for his distraught mother, Patti Stallings. She not only lost her child to a deadly ailment, but was also jailed for his alleged murder.

allowed to see him for an hour a week. And they were forbidden to feed him.

But on one visit, Patti was briefly left alone with her son — and a bottle of baby-milk. A little later, when others were in the same room, she fed Ryan his milk.

Five days later, the baby was back in hospital, diagnosed as having ethylene glycol poisoning. Patti was arrested at once and charged with assault. Her husband kept watch by their son's hospital cot. "He was lying there with tubes in his arms and throat, blowing up like a balloon," Dave recalls. "I couldn't stand it."

On 7 September baby Ryan died in his father's arms. At the Stallings' home, police found a bottle of anti-freeze. Patti was charged with first-degree murder.

"I couldn't sleep," she says. "I lost a huge amount of weight. Only my husband's support, and my Buddhist religion, kept me from going insane."

After a month held in jail, Patti discovered she was pregnant. The new baby, David Junior, was born in February 1990. He was taken from his mother and put in a foster home. Not for the first time, Patti Stallings broke down and wept.

Within days, Patti was told her new baby had been vomiting and breathing unnaturally. "They were the same things that had been wrong with Ryan," she says. "I went into shock."

Tests showed that David Junior had a rare genetic disorder called methylmalomic acidemia, or MMA — which can create its own poisons. It affects one in every 48,000 babies, and few live beyond eight years old.

Patti's lawyers called on the prosecutors to look into the possibility that baby Ryan had died of the same ailment. Patti was let out on bail while the police investigated.

But the murder trial went ahead. Doctors claimed that whether or not Ryan was born with MMA, what killed him was a dose of anti-freeze.

Patti went on trial in January 1991. Doctors and scientists

testified that the human body could not make ethylene glycol. The defence tried to show the similarities of Ryan's and his brother's symptoms. Judge Gary Kramer would not allow that evidence because no experts were called to back it up.

Police and social workers claimed Patti seemed cold and uncaring when told her son had died. But the most damning testimony came from tests showing that the bottle Patti had used on her visit to Ryan in the foster home contained traces of ethylene glycol – even though it had been washed and filled again since her visit.

A tearful Patti told the jury she had not worn a coat or carried a handbag on her visit, so would have had nowhere to hide any poison. "I don't know how they think I did it," she said. "I'm just as confused as anyone else in this room."

Defence lawyer Eric Rathbone suggested that another relative might have killed Ryan – or that poison could have got into his body by some other mysterious means. The jury debated the evidence for 10 hours. Then they found Patti guilty. She was jailed for life, with no parole.

Even then, the nightmare was not complete. Social workers decided to take baby David Junior away from his father, on the grounds that Dave Stallings had "abandoned" the child. In fact, Dave said, lawyer Rathbone had advised him not to see his baby.

Patti appealed against the jury's verdict, claiming that Rathbone had made a mess of her defence. The State ruled that she had been let down by her lawyer and ordered her to be freed on $60,000 bail, to await a fresh trial. And a senior university scientist who had been reading about the case also took a hand.

William Sly, chairman of St Louis University's biochemistry department, suspected that baby Ryan, like his brother, might have been born with MMA – and could have died from it. Sly arranged for tests to be done on frozen samples of Ryan's blood serum. They showed that the original reports of deadly amounts of ethylene glycol in the blood had been incorrect.

More tests were done by Yale University genetics professor Dr Piero Rinaldo. He proved that MMA had indeed killed Ryan.

The make-up of poisons produced by the disease, he explained, is similar to that of ethylene glycol. But the earlier findings were "grossly inaccurate and probably preconceived". Rinaldo said, "I've never seen such lousy work."

On 20 September last year Patti Stallings was freed. State prosecutor George McElroy made a public apology. "We can't undo the suffering the Stallings have endured," he said, "but I hope they will be happier in the future."

Patti, a former shop assistant, and Dave, a plate engraver, have launched multi-million-pound lawsuits against two hospitals, three doctors and a laboratory firm. But, Patti claims, she is not bitter. "The anger and rage and all that — it's ugly," she says. "I want to move on. We just want to quietly go on with our lives."

And there is still the uphill battle of sick little Dave Junior. Patti has to feed him by a tube into his stomach. That takes special patience because the MMA makes it hard for him to digest proteins. And he's so frail, even a cold could kill him.

"Taking care of David is going to be a whole new fight," Patti says. "But we are used to fighting."

19

Murder They Wrote
Bloodbath in Beverly Hills

The brutal murder of Jose and Kitty Menendez shook their wealthy Beverly Hills community to its core. Seven months later, parents rich and poor were united in shock at the two sons' arrest. Had Erik and Lyle slaughtered their parents for money?

Hollywood scriptwriters would have been hard pressed to come up with as shocking a case as the "Murder They Wrote" scandal that's rocked America. On the balmy night of August 20, 1989, multi-millionaire movie mogul Jose Menendez, 45, and his ex-beauty-queen wife Kitty, 44, were cold-bloodedly gunned down in the library of their beautiful Beverly Hills mansion.

The handsome, hardworking couple were relaxing in front of the TV, eating strawberries and cream, when they were blasted with pump-action shotguns at point-blank range. Jose, in shorts and sweatshirt, almost had his head blown off when shot from behind with a 12-gauge shotgun. The crazed killers pumped four more slugs into him to make sure he was dead — one of them through his mouth. His wife Kitty, still in her jogging clothes, was riddled with 10 wounds from another shotgun, leading police to believe that more than one person was involved in the shocking outrage. She had been shot all over, but the four blasts aimed at her face left her unrecognisable.

At first police suspected that Mafia hitmen or even Fidel Castro's henchmen were responsible for the awful slaughter — Jose had dealt with a video company linked to the Mob, and the Cuban-born tycoon was known to hate the dictator's regime. But homicide experts soon rejected the theory of professional assassins, as the murder was too messy.

After seven months, the victims' two sons Lyle, 22, and Erik, 19, both college tennis champs, were suddenly arrested and charged. The dashing duo weren't even major suspects at first, even though Erik, with Lyle's help, had penned a screenplay called *The Perfect Murder*. It involved the far-fetched tale of a sadistic 18-year-old who kills his rich parents to inherit a $200 million fortune.

Police discovered the amateurish 61-page script during an intense manhunt for the vicious killers. It had been carefully written just two months before the real-life murders and, in a bizarre twist, Erik's mother had helped to type it. It described how "The door opens, exposing the luxurious suite and Mr and Mrs Cromwell lying in bed. 'Good evening Mother, good evening Father.' Hamilton's voice is of attempted compassion but the hatred completely overwhelms it. Their faces are of questioning horror as he closes the door gently. The scene fades and the murder is left to the imagination of the audience."

Murder investigators were at first unwilling to suspect the boys, as they found it hard to believe that the "loving" but often wayward kids could have committed such a horrific and callous crime. The Menendeze's owned a sprawling $3 million eight-bedroom mansion on Elm Drive, Beverly Hills, and the luxurious home, complete with its own swimming pool and tennis court, could count Elton John, Michael Jackson and also Prince as former occupiers. The couple's happiness and wealth had made them the envy of Tinseltown and their gory deaths came as a brutal shock.

Beverly Hills police chief Marvin Iannone said: "I have been in this business for 33 years, and I know of few murders that were more savage. But who knows what goes on in families? It seems the boys may have acted out their screenplay for real."

There was no evidence of burglary at their heavily fortified mansion which had the latest in high-tech security alarms.

Erik Menedez (*left*) with brother Lyle (*right*), wrote a
screenplay, 'The Perfect Murder'. Its improbable plot had a son
killing his rich parents for cash. They are pictured here with
their parents.

The boys said they found the fortress-like iron gate open and the front door unlocked. "They shot and killed my parents," wailed Lyle, between sobs, to the emergency number as Erik made the chilling screams in the background. "I don't know what happened. Didn't hear anything. I just got home. Erik, shut up. Get away from them."

Lyle and Erik, who were as thick as thieves, claimed they'd gone to see the Bond movie *Licence To Kill* on that fateful night but couldn't get in and went to see *Batman* instead. They did not have any ticket stubs. Then they visited a Santa Monica food festival where they rang a friend. No trace was ever found of the call.

The two sons at first seemed to be heartbroken and had help from Jerome Oziel, a psychologist, to get over the trauma. Said Erik, "I've never seen anything like it, never will see anything like it. They looked like wax. I've never seen Dad look so helpless, it's sad to think he ever would be. He came to the US from Cuba when he was 16, without his father — at almost the same age when Lyle and I don't have a dad."

But there was a hint from their shrink's notes that everything was not all rosy. "My dad really could not do something well enough," said Lyle. "It was very hard for Erik and me — I had arguments with him all the time and I rarely won." Yet within a few weeks their mourning seemed to be over as the boys lived it up on a $3 million life insurance policy taken out by their dad. Lyle bought a $40,000 red Porsche Carrera convertible car, a $1,000,000 apartment and a $10,000 Rolex watch. His shopping sprees included five silk shirts snapped up in several minutes. Lyle then quit Princeton University in New Jersey and paid $300,000 for a local restaurant, called Chuck's Spring Street Cafe.

Renaming it Mr Buffalo's, he planned to form a nationwide chain and also dabbled in real estate and showbiz. He tried unsuccessfully to become a promoter of a Soul II Soul concert.

Meanwhile little brother Erik, once a top US tennis junior, turned down a chance to go to the prestigious University of California and tried to make it as a tennis pro. He moved into an elegant apartment and hired a full-time private coach at $30,000 a year.

The Menendez sons' spending alerted the police. What they uncovered were two spoiled rich kids who would lie, cheat and steal to get all they wanted. At 17, Erik was arrested for breaking into two houses in LA and stealing a safe from one and $55,000 worth of cash and jewellery from the other. He got off with probation after his father paid damages to the victims. Lyle was suspected of involvement but Erik took the rap as he was a minor and so likely to get off with a light sentence. Big brother was just as bad. Lyle was suspended for the year in his first term at university when his class report was nearly an exact copy of a classmate's. He flaunted his wealth at high school and was know as "Lyle the Loanshark", cruising clubs and showing off his red Alfa Romeo. He was also suspended twice from driving as he hadn't paid his parking tickets, so he was chauffeured in a luxury limousine at Dad's expense.

Their best mate Reed Newhall remembers they were "very competitive". He says: "Erik was verbally aggressive. If he didn't get his own way, Lyle would swear or bat a ball over the wall in disgust, a bit like John McEnroe in one of his tantrums."

Soon after the murders, Erik said: "There was a lot of pressure to become great. We are prototypes of my father — he wanted us to be exactly like him. My father hated Fidel Castro with a passion and wanted to spend the rest of his life getting him out of Cuba. He probably would have done it and probably would have been assassinated somewhere down the line.

"My brother wants to become President of the US but I want to be Senator, and be with the people of Cuba. I'm not going to live for my father, but I think his dreams are what I want to achieve. I feel he's in me, pushing me." The boys were driven to succeed by a father who rose from dishwashing to get through college to a young, successful businessman and a mother who was a national swimming champ.

When Jose won a scholarship to the University of Illinois, he met Kitty Anderson, a former beauty queen of a nearby town. Jose got a degree in accounting and quickly made his fortune. After working for RCA, where he signed Duran Duran and the Eurythmics, he moved to the subsidiary of the company that produced the *Rambo* films with Sylvester Stallone. Friends included Barry Manilow and Kenny Rogers.

Jose was so rich, he was spending $10 million on doing up his new mansion on elegant Mulholland Drive, which is down the road from Marlon Brando and Jack Nicholson, while he still lived in his old house. But his co-worker Ralph King said, "Despite the pressures of work, he always had time for his children."

"His executive job took him into some dodgy deals with tough tycoons. One firm that sued him was a distributor of porn films with Mafia ties, while the owner of a record chain bought by the company was a convicted extortionist. Homicide cops thought the killings were linked to Jose's recent takeovers, but soon Erik and Lyle were nailed to the nightmare on Elm Drive by circumstantial evidence and confession tapes that may be banned from being used in evidence.

Although the police had read Erik's screenplay, the first real break came when a shotgun shell casing was found in Lyle's jacket. Then cops discovered that a file reference to a new will had been erased "by mistake" on Jose's home computer by Lyle. The old will left the $9 million estate to his sons. A police spokesman said: "We believe the parents were going to cut them out of the will because they were out of control, and that's why they were killed."

Erik's friend Craig Cignarelli then claimed that Erik had confessed to the murder in private − Erik denies this. The murder weapons were never found but two 12-gauge shotguns were bought at a nearby store two days before the massacre under the name of Donovan Goodreau, once a roommate of Lyle's, who'd had his driver's licence stolen.

Erik was charged on his return from a tennis tournament.

Their attorney claims that conversations between a psychologist and his client are "privileged" and so cannot be used in a court of law. While the two sons are held in county jail their trial's been set for later this year. And they still claim they're innocent. They've found an ally in Jose's 72- year-old mother, Maria. "They couldn't have done such a thing," she says. "They loved their parents very much. The boys cried to me when they realised they had lost them. I don't know who killed them. All I know is that it wasn't Erik and Lyle."

If the boys are found guilty, it's ironic that their true-life murder story is much more horrific than any of those violent video scripts dreamt up by their father's parent company.

20

Presumed Innocent
A wife-killer's tears that fooled the world

When wealthy Charles Stuart was pulled out from his car with a serious bullet wound, his pregnant wife dying beside him, America was outraged by the brutal attack. Months later the horrific truth was discovered – yuppie Stuart was a man so bent by money and ambition that he slaughtered his own family.

"My wife's been shot – I've been shot!" These chilling words marked the beginning of a gory murder that mystified and horrified America. The dashing yuppie Charles Stuart was speaking to police on his car phone, telling them that his pregnant wife Carol had been shot next to him and he was bleeding to death from a horrific stomach wound.

Driving through the streets, looking for help, Stuart was able to remain on the phone long enough for police patrol cars to track him down and save his life – only for him to kill himself two months later.

Stuart, a 29-year-old manager of a posh fur shop in Boston, claimed that a 'black mugger wearing a track suit and baseball cap' had hijacked their car just as they were leaving their pre-natal classes. The gravel-voiced gunman had supposedly robbed them of jewellery and cash – then opened fire and left them in their car for dead.

Although Carol died within hours of a massive gunshot wound to the back of her head, her baby, Christopher, was delivered by Caesarean section, born eight weeks premature and weighing only 3lb 13 oz. After clinging to life for 17 days, the tragic tot also died and the nation wept once more. Although he was still in agony following two life-saving

Yuppie Love - Charles and Carol Stuart were the perfect couple - or so it seemed. Beneath the sheen of high powered jobs and costly houses lay charmer Chuck's growing resentment of Carol's plans.

Top: 'Good night sweet wife, I love you' read Charles's farewell to Carol. Brother Matthew, second from the left in foreground, agonised before he went to the police.

Above: Shelley Yandoli and brother Michael Stuart during a news conference about Charles Stuart's plan to kill Carol.

operations, Stuart insisted on being taken to another hospital to cradle baby Christopher in his arms as he died.

Stuart's touching farewell message to Carol was read out at his wife's funeral, to some 800 mourners, including the Massachusetts Governor — Michael Dukakis. "Good night, sweet wife, my love," it said. "Now you sleep away from me. I will never again know the feeling of your hand in mine, but I will always feel you.

"I miss you and I love you. God has called you to His hands, not to take you away from me but to bring you away from the cruelty and the violence that fill this world."

Two months later, just as it looked like a cold-blooded psychopath was about to get away scot-free, the terrible truth behind the double murder suddenly emerged.

Greedy Charlie, who enjoyed every luxury that his $80,000 salary could afford, had killed his wife to get his hands on even more money — several six-figure insurance policies. One of these had been taken out just weeks before her death.

With police on the verge of arresting callous Charlie, he parked his flashy new car on the Tobin Bridge in Boston and plunged 200 feet to his death in the murky River Mystic. The suicide note he left in his car said simply: "I love my family. The last four months have been hell."

Now the incredible murder story is being turned into a controversial TV movie, with Stuart played by hunky *Thirtysomething* star Ken Olin. Sexy newcomer Annabella Price will play the part of beautiful brunette Carol Stuart.

Amazingly, the real-life drama was caught on film when a TV crew working with the Boston police just happened to be on the scene when the Stuarts were being pulled from their car. The press were also on the scene, having followed the police patrol cars trying for 15 minutes to trace their Toyota Maxima. Charles had claimed that he could not see the street signs because he was too weak from loss of blood to turn the car lights on — even though they were only under the steering wheel.

While the Stuarts were being rushed to the hospital, he

asked over and over again, "How is my wife?" But the heartless killer only wanted to make sure that she was dead.

Former altar-boy Stuart was never a suspect in the investigation until the day before his death. Says Boston District Attorney Thomas Mundy: "It might seem unusual for a mugger to jump into a car and shoot two people. But then it's even more unbelievable that a man whose only vice is playing hockey on Wednesday nights, who works 52 hours a week and makes a large salary, who friends said was enthralled with his wife and baby, would shoot her. And then shoot himself so seriously that the bullet would almost kill him." Stuart was in intensive care for 10 days followed by six weeks in hospital with damage to his bowels, gall bladder and liver − he had to wear a colostomy bag after his operations. Police think that Stuart panicked and shot himself in the stomach by mistake while aiming for his foot.

In the wake of Stuart's death was left a city seething with racial tension because innocent black men had come within hours of being charged with the murders. And tension was already high in the weeks after the brutal crime as hundreds of black men were stopped by police and questioned in an attempt to prevent more murderous attacks.

Stuart's suicide prompted an investigation into his personal life that soon revealed his sordid history of devious lying, cheating and also womanising. He'd even bragged to his friends on nights out that he'd had an affair with pretty university graduate Deborah Allen, although she has since denied it.

"There will never be any evidence of romantic involvement between us," she said in a statement through her lawyer.

Smoothie Stuart came from the nearby wealthy town of Revere but had lied when he'd talked his way into a job at the top people's store Kakas by claiming that he went to a good university on a sports scholarship. After Stuart's death plunge, and on learning of his lies, the owners of Kakas checked the safe and found that a .38 snub-nose revolver was missing. There has never been any concrete evidence that Chuck, as he liked to be known, pulled the trigger that ended two lives, but circumstantial evidence is now overwhelming.

The man who turned Stuart's image from heroic victim into heartless villain was his own younger brother, Matthew, who had helped hide vital evidence — including the apparent murder weapon. Stuart took his life the day after he learned that paint-mixer Matthew had told police what he really knew about the grisly events on the night of October 13, 1989.

After a dry run the day before, Chuck met his brother at a prearranged place in the Boston neighbourhood of Mission Hill to carry out an "insurance scam" — for which he would be paid $6,000. Chuck pulled up and threw Carol's Gucci handbag, containing her wallet and jewellery, and a .38 calibre gun, into Matthew's car. Matthew drove off and hurled all the incriminating evidence into the Revere River, but kept Carol's expensive engagement ring — which he later gave to police to prove his terrible story.

Matthew says that he did see something in the seat next to his brother but didn't realise that it might have been Carol and that his brother was wounded. He claims that he knew nothing of his sister-in-law's murder until later that same night. Under an old Massachusetts law, he can't be charged with trying to conceal the crime as it was carried out by a member of his own family. He only went to the police when, 71 days after the murder, a black man called William Bennett, who had a long history of armed robbery, was about to be charged with the killing. Chuck had hoped to frame Bennett by picking him out of a police line-up saying that he "most looked like" the gunman he'd seen.

"The line-up pushed Matthew over the brink," says his lawyer. "He had agonised over it for weeks." Ironically, Bennett's picture in the paper was recognised by one of his real victims and he was charged for robbing a shop at gunpoint.

A police probe revealed that for months Chuck had been plotting to kill his wife. He had even tried to hire an old friend, David MacClean, to do the murderous job. "He asked me, 'Can you take care of my wife — you know, kill her?' " says MacClean. "It was very business-like, almost like a board meeting. He didn't want to spend the rest of his life breaking his back for somebody else. His wife refused to have an abortion and he was afraid that she would not return to her job when the baby was born."

Stuart also allegedly arranged with Matthew to break into his house and make it look like a robbery had been committed, so he could kill her and blame it on burglars. A few days before the murder the calculating killer had even dropped into a local restaurant to confirm a reservation for a party, setting up his image as the devoted husband. The Driftwood restaurant owner Jim Hogan remembers: "He sat there talking about how he was going to have a Christmas baby, and how excited they were about coming to the party — and all the time he knew she wasn't going to make it. She was going to be dead."

On 13 October, Chuck took Carol for a romantic break at a charming country inn in Connecticut so that they could celebrate their fourth wedding anniversary. They acted like young lovers but Chuck had already set the wheels in motion to end what friends and family thought was the perfect marriage, with one gunshot.

The couple met and fell in love in 1980 when Chuck was a short-order cook at the Driftwood and Carol got a part-time job as a waitress. With similar working-class backgrounds and with dreams of a better life, they bought themselves a beautiful four-bedroom house in the well-to-do town of Reading, where he was a very popular man in the community. There was no hint that behind the facade lay a merciless killer. "My children loved having Chuck over to baby-sit," says a neighbour.

Their $100,000 mortgage kept the couple on a tight budget but Carol desperately wanted a baby and she was overjoyed when she got pregnant. Carol told her family, "I know it's a boy. It's Christopher." Still, the only real crack in their marriage appeared to be Chuck's boozy nights out with the lads on a Friday. Maureen Vajdic, their bridesmaid, says, "Carol told Chuck, 'Don't you have any concern for me at all? I'm pregnant. These late nights will have to stop when the baby's born.'"

There was also an unconfirmed report that Stuart was taking money from his company, and even a suggestion that he had gone into a clinic to fight a cocaine problem. But on the surface, everything seemed fine.

What drove Stuart to kill his wife? His friends think it was overwhelming ambition that drove him to work so hard and that, ironically, also drove him to kill the people he should have loved most. The prospect of a baby in the family had made him fear for his lavish lifestyle. Until he became a home owner, the exceedingly vain Stuart wore $500 suits and dyed his hair. He dined at the best restaurants, and went on expensive holidays with his wife. David MacClean reveals, "He dreamed of owning his own restaurant and realised that he could not afford it on his income alone."

The whole truth about the private world of this cold-hearted killer may have gone down with Stuart to his watery grave, but the closest thing to a confession of guilt could be his farewell letter to Carol. "We must know that God's will was done. We must forgive the sinner, because He would."

Actor Ken Olin sees Stuart as a terrible symbol of the insatiable greed inherent in the yuppie culture of the '80s. "He just took it to the extreme. And then he outlived the decade by just four days."

21

Over the Top

The panoramic view from the clifftop overlooking the ocean was spectacular. Bride-to-be Deana Wild, 20, looked on in wide-eyed wonder for a few minutes. Then she took a few careful steps forward and peered over the edge at the waves crashing onto the granite rocks 400 feet below.

It was Big Sur at its most beautiful — one of America's seven natural wonders. This picturesque stretch of northern Californian coastline, with its huge surfer waves, thick redwood forests and mountainous range, attracts thousands of tourists each year.

One second Deana was enjoying the scenery, overlooking Seal Beach, and the next she was hurtling to her death. One of her high-heeled shoes was found on the top of the cliff while the other was discovered 50 feet below on a narrow ledge just before a sheer drop to the Pacific Ocean. Did she jump? Did she trip? Or was she pushed?

Her future in-laws, Virginia, 55, and husband Billie Joe McGinnis, 53, heard Deana's screams and the sickening thud as her body bounced like a rag doll when she hit rock bottom. They told police they didn't see what happened because they were walking back to their car. But they gave police 12 snapshots they had taken moments before Deana's plunge, including one photo with Billie Joe's hand on her back.

The spot she'd fallen from was known locally as "lover's leap" because many distraught people had jumped to their deaths there. After police conducted an exhaustive investigation, they ruled Deana's death on 2 April, 1987, a tragic accident — even though the coroner's report left the verdict as "pending".

But Deana's mother Bobbie Roberts couldn't believe that her retarded daughter, who had the IQ of a 10-year-old and was naive and trusting, would kill herself or even risk her life by stepping too close to the edge. After all, according to the McGinnis duo, she had everything to live for.

After a brief marriage, Deana had fallen head over heels in love again, and was engaged to James Coates, Virginia's son by her first marriage. This was despite the fact that Deana had not finalised her divorce, and her intended was in prison for second-degree murder. Deana had been staying with the McGinnises at their home near San Diego, California. They appeared to get along fine. So well, in fact, they'd taken that fateful trip together 500 miles up the coast.

Bobbie Roberts had taken out a £1,500 burial policy on Deana to pay for funeral bills, just in case of a tragic accident. But after her daughter's death, she had trouble claiming it. So she turned to an old family friend, lawyer Steve Keeney, to get to the bottom of it. "I promised Bobbie I would find the truth," says Keeney. "Right from the start, nothing fell into place. First the case did not pass the 'smell test' of the coroner's office, which never gave a cause of death.

"And the more we learned about Virginia's background the more we learned about the case facts."

Over a period of two years he uncovered a shocking catalogue of potential crimes in Virginia's past − including the possibility of murder − that had gone virtually unnoticed by police. Over two decades, Virginia had made seven insurance claims for fire, all suspected arson cases. One claim paid out £80,000. She'd lived in houses in Kentucky, New York and California that had all burned down.

Virginia met her first husband, neighbour Richard Coates, when he was watching a fire at her parents' barn in New York. But he divorced her after two more mysterious fires at their homes. In 1985, Virginia insured a truck she had rented while moving house. It was stolen along with many

116

items from her home. The truck was later found burned out.

Keeney discovered an even more shocking secret buried in her past. In April 1972, Virginia's three-year-old daughter Cynthia died in an accident in Louisville, Kentucky. She was playing on top of a tractor in a barn when she jumped off, hanging herself on some loose twine. Virginia told friends that she got £600 in insurance after Cynthia died.

Police sergeant Robert Jones, who conducted the investigation and still has the deadly twine, says, "I always had my suspicions about Cynthia's death but there was no proof of foul play at the time." No autopsy was performed. But he's recently had the body exhumed so a battery of tests can be carried out. "We're looking for strangulation marks, fractures or some sort of poisoning."

In 1974, Virginia's second husband Sylvester Rearden died of cancer. But police have discovered that Virginia was nursing him and giving him medication. Three months later a blaze burned the house down.

A few months before Deana fell, Virginia's mother Mary Hoffman, died – officially of a heart problem. But Virginia, who lived with her, was helping to give her insulin for diabetes. A family friend told police that Virginia had talked about how insulin could be used to kill somebody without raising any suspicion. The friend also said Virginia had told her Mary had talked one day about "not living very long". The next day she was dead.

Police are also probing her death. "We are looking into any death that Virginia has been present at or associated with," said an official.

Bobbie Roberts believed hers was the only insurance policy on Deana's life. But Keeney unearthed another one. On 1 April, 1987 – the day before the tragedy – the McGinnis duo took out an insurance policy on Deana's life.

State Farm insurance agent Mac McCain told Keeney that he had an uneasy feeling about Virginia. As she was leaving the office she turned and asked, "Does this policy cover accidental death?" Deana signed the policy, not knowing she was virtually signing her death certificate. Virginia paid the first premium of £40.

McCain knew that Virginia had made several claims against his company and balked at approving the policy. So he sent it to head office to let them decide. A company spokesman said: "What could we tell Deana? 'We can't insure you as we believe there's a possibility you're going to be murdered?'"

Two weeks later Virginia came back to the office, tossed the policy on the desk and said, "She's dead." The signature of Deana's neighbour had been forged on the £22,000 policy. The major beneficiary was Deana's jailed fiancé James Coates. The other beneficiaries were Virginia and Billie Joe, who later divorced.

Tests show that Deana had taken the anti-depressant Elavil, for which Billie Joe had a prescription at the time. Deana's mum says, "Physically, it could make a person very drowsy, so Deana wouldn't have been aware of what was going on."

The mounting circumstantial evidence was enough to convince police to charge the couple with murder. But while awaiting trial, Billie Joe died in prison of AIDS.

District Attorney Luis Aragon said in his opening statement that "this was murder, not an accident". He claimed the couple drugged Deana and gave her a shove over the cliff. The insurance policy was "the smoking gun" that tied the plot together.

But defence attorney Albert Tamayo said: "There are bound to be suspicions where an insurance policy's bought one day and a fall occurs on the next. But it doesn't prove murder." He claimed Deana had somehow slipped in her high heels.

During the seven-week trial, a makeshift courtroom was set up on the majestic cliff overlooking Seal Beach so that the jury could get an idea first-hand of what happened. Tamayo said, "It was a unique experience. The judge said it was a most spectacular courtroom and I tend to agree with him."

Juror Peter Young said the bus trip from the Monterey courtroom to Big Sur was crucial in visualising what happened that day. Juror Jim Allender reckoned it was unlikely that a person could have slipped from the point where Deana fell.

Virginia McGinnis was found guilty of murder in the first degree. She was also found guilty of conspiracy, insurance fraud and forgery. She was sentenced to life without any chance of parole.

Deana's mum said, "I'm elated. This is the best day I've had in five years." Virginia may also face murder charges connected to the death hanging of her daughter Cynthia.

22

Rivals in Love — One Had to Die

Farmer Bill Buss, 26, couldn't believe his luck when two beautiful women — one a princess, the other a queen — battled for his hand in marriage. But the dream turned into a nightmare when 21-year-old dairy princess, Lori Esker — heartbroken by Bill's rejection of her after a year-long affair — strangled homecoming queen Lisa Cihaski, 21.

Lovely Lisa's lifeless body was found by her distraught mother who'd gone looking for her when she failed to come home late at night. The grisly murder horrified residents of tiny, tightly-knit farming communities Birnamwood and Hatley in Wisconsin — the dairy heartland of America. They were terrified a madman was on the loose and, for the first time in their lives, locked their doors at night.

But eight days after the killing, on Wednesday, 20 September last year, they were in for an even bigger shock. The newly crowned dairy princess was charged with her former classmate's murder. To add to the heartache, Lori and Lisa's mothers had gone to school together and were "best of friends".

At first Lori denied the murder, but after being quizzed three times by cops she confessed that she'd killed Lisa "by accident" while begging her to give Bill up. She said that a life-and-death struggle broke out between them when Esker suggested that she was pregnant by Buss. As they wrestled, Lori claimed that she grabbed a belt from the back seat of the car, wrapped it round Lisa's neck and tightened it. When Lisa's body went limp, Lori took out a mirror from her rival's bag and held it to her face to see if she was breathing. "When I realised that she wasn't, I thought to myself, 'Oh my God, I killed her.' I didn't mean to hurt her. I know Lisa knows that." Nevertheless she pulled a ring off Lisa's finger because she thought "maybe Bill gave it to her". When police asked Bill if Lisa had any enemies, he replied "only Lori". The police — who didn't believe it was a case of self-defence — claimed Lori's fatal attraction for Bill led to her hatching a deadly plot.

Blonde-haired Lori, president of the local Future Farmers of America organisation, was the first woman in rural Marathon County history to be charged with killing another woman. The packed trial was told that Esker was so infatuated with Bill, that when he told her he was engaged to Lisa, she refused to believe it was over and begged him to marry her instead.

Bill had been dating Lisa for three years when she told him she needed "some space". He began seeing Lori and admitted, "I loved her and I really cared about her. We had a romantic and sexual relationship." But when his ex-girlfriend found out, she became jealous and wanted him back. Bill obliged. The day he saw Lisa again, a devastated Lori rang him in a rage, saying, "How could you do this to me?"

Buss told the court that although she looked like a fragile beauty, Lori had grown up on a 350-acre farm and was strong enough to handle tough farm chores. The implication was that she was strong enough to strangle another woman. The last time they had spoken by phone was just three days before the murder. Lori told him, "I just want you to know that I have accepted the fact that you and Lisa are back together, now I'm going to leave you alone."

But that phone call was her first step in an evil murder plot. The day of the murder, Lori left a message on a friend's answerphone saying, "I just called to talk. I'm going to the library to study." The prosecutor said it was a weak attempt to create an alibi. Lori drove to where Lisa worked and waited until she came out.

Strangled Homecoming queen Lisa Cihaski, aged 21.

Top: Esker was so infatuated with 26 yr old Bill that when he told her he was engaged to Lisa she refused to believe it was finally over.

Below: Victim's gravestone.

The jury took seven hours to find Lori guilty of pre-planned murder. She was sentenced to life in prison but could be paroled by the age of 34. When sentenced, she broke down and wept as she said: "If I could trade places with Lisa, I would. I'll be punishing myself for as long as I live."

23

Debts Drove Dad to Drown Kids

It had been a tiring day. Mum and Dad trailing the four kids from one furniture store to the next, checking the prices of beds for the new house. For Larry DeLisle, 30, it had gone on too long and he was glad that now at last they were heading home.

In the back of the 12-year-old car, the two older kids — Brian, eight, and Melissa, four — ate their ice-creams on that hot August day in 1989, chattering and laughing away with their little sisters — Kathryn, two, and eight-month-old baby Emily.

But all of a sudden those screams of laughter turned into screams of terror as their car roared out of control, smashed through a dead-end barrier and plunged into the river.

Larry DeLisle struggled free and swam to safety. So did his wife. But the children all drowned.

In the working-class Detroit suburb of Wyandotte, the public flocked to dead-end Eureka Street to lay bouquets next to pictures of the victims, devastated by the tragedy.

"To have four beautiful babies one minute and the next they're gone," Larry DeLisle told local TV. "If you think about that all the time, you might as well put on a straitjacket."

But how did this tragedy happen? DeLisle, a store manager, explained to police that his accelerator pedal had stuck and, at the same moment, he had suffered cramp in his leg. His 33-year-old wife Suzanne, he added, had tried to turn off the ignition and take the car out of gear.

Police ran routine checks and soon discovered a sinister background of financial and emotional troubles. Larry

Top: Screams of joy soon turned into complete terror for (*from left*) Kathryn, Melissa, Brian and Emily DeLisle.

Above left: Suzanne, 33, stuck by husband Larry, 30. 'If I thought for a second he was guilty, I'd be out screaming louder than anyone to convict him,' she declared.

Above right: Larry DeLisle decided to end it all and take his family with him. But when he ran his car off the road and into a river he decided to swim to safety. His kids weren't so lucky.

Top: William DeLisle reaches out to his wife Helen and mourners after leaving a memorial service for his four grand nieces and nephews.

Below: District Court Officer, Randy Miller, escorts Larry DeLisle, 28, after he appeared mute before Judge Lawrence L.Emmett.

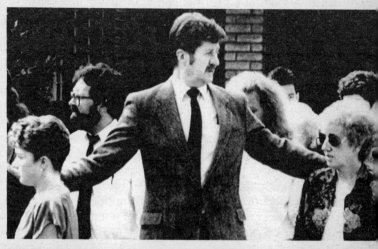

DeLisle was up to his eyes in debt. On credit cards alone, he owed $10,000. Though he took home around $300 a week, he had to hand over 90 per cent of that to Suzanne.

To help solve his money worries, DeLisle's Uncle Bill had given them a rent-free home. But Suzanne just spent all of their money on things for the house, including new beds.

Detectives also discovered that the family's 12-year-old car had been left to Larry 18 months earlier by his father . . . who had shot himself in its front seat. Blood stains from the suicide were still there.

The car was tested for mechanical failure. Out of 20 trial runs, the accelerator did stick — just once. But why had DeLisle turned down that dead end anyway? And, even if the accelerator was sticking and the driver did have a sudden cramp, why didn't he try braking? Or swerving the wheel right or left, instead of charging straight down into the river?

Police came to the conclusion that DeLisle had attempted to murder his entire family and commit suicide — but that he chickened out of his own death at the last moment, never considering the possibility that Suzanne might swim clear too.

DeLisle agreed to a lie-detector test. "I had a little leg cramp," he said. "I just couldn't seem to slam on the brakes. I didn't want to. I don't know why."

But then he began what sounded like a confession . . . "I just wanted to scare my wife enough. Slam on the brakes, come to a standstill. Get her all upset so that she'd forget about beds for a couple of days and just let me be. I couldn't stop the car accelerating. I didn't want to stop it.

"I didn't mean to hurt my babies. I love my wife. I didn't even realise they were in the car. My mind went blank. I really hate that car. My father blew his brains out in it. And he didn't even say goodbye . . ."

DeLisle's job, too, had got on top of him. "I just wanted it to be over. The constant repetition. Same thing, day after day. I wanted to be closer to my wife. I don't deserve to live. Gas chamber, electrocution, hang me. I don't care. Just throw away the key."

DeLisle was charged with four murders, and sympathy for him soon turned to hatred. During pre-trial hearings other parents screamed, "Killer! Scum! Drown the man!"

Suzanne DeLisle stuck by her husband. "If I thought for a second he was guilty," she declared, "I'd be screaming louder than anyone to convict him." Giving evidence, she tried to explain away the fact that the car had not turned away from the river. She said that she was pulling the wheel to the left — and her husband was trying to pull to the right.

But her testimony contained a damning giveaway. Though she had told police her husband's foot had stayed jammed to the floor, she now said that a split second before the crash, he took it off the accelerator.

Also, the night before the tragedy, and again earlier on the day of the alleged murders, DeLisle had been seen driving along Eureka Street. So he knew it was a dead end.

DeLisle was found guilty. Judge Columbo sentenced the bereaved father to life in jail, with no parole. DeLisle has appealed for a new trial, claiming that police "hypnotised" him. And wife Suzanne plans to stand by him to the bitter end. "He's not guilty," she weeps. "I think about him every minute of the day."

24

Slaughter of the Innocents

Sobbing and screaming, the panic-stricken mother dashed into the hospital, her small son in her arms. "He's stopped breathing!" she shrieked. Doctors rushed four-year-old Jose Antonio Lumbrera into the emergency room of St Catherine's Hospital. But an hour later, the child was dead.

The boy's mother, 32-year-old Diana Lumbrera, seemed inconsolable. She broke down and, between bouts of helpless sobbing, blurted out a tragic tale. All her other children, she told the nurses, had also died young. All five of them.

On the day of Jose's funeral, as his mother wept piteously at the graveside, a pathologist back at the hospital in Garden City, Kansas, was doing a post-mortem on the boy. Jose, the expert decided, had probably been suffocated by someone.

The police began to look into Diana Lumbrera's past. She had not lived long in Garden City. Her home had been the tiny farming town of Bovina, in neighbouring Texas. It was there, on 30 November, 1976, that Diana — then 18-year-old Mrs Garza — ran into Parmer County Hospital carrying the lifeless body of three-month-old Joanna Garza, her second child by husband Lionel Garza. Doctors certified death by "strangulation due to convulsive disorder". There was no post-mortem.

Fifteen months later, in February 1978, she turned up at another hospital, the West Texas Medical Center in Lubbock — carrying her small son, Jose Lionel Garza. He was 10 weeks old and she said, "very sick".

Jose Lionel was treated successfully for pneumonia. And

after three days he was well enough to be moved out of the intensive care unit. But before he could be transferred, there was sudden drama in the unit. Diana Lumbrera came rushing out, screaming that something had happened to her baby.

Jose Lionel was dead. Dr John Rankin, who had been treating him, ordered a post-mortem. But it failed to pinpoint how the baby had died. Jose Lionel was marked down as a victim of Sudden Infant Death Syndrome — cot death.

"Two or three nurses were on duty in the unit," Dr Rankin says now. "But because of the layout, patients were not fully within sight at all times. It was a bit unusual to have a patient who's been improving, with no fever, suddenly stop living. But I had to accept it at the time, on the objective evidence."

And, of course, Jose's mother had conveniently not told Dr Rankin about the equally sudden death of little Joanna.

About eight months later, it happened once more. Into Parmer County Hospital rushed Diana Lumbrera, yet again, this time with her three-year-old daughter Melissa. The child was already dead. Again doctors performed a post-mortem to try to discover the exact cause of her death. Their paperwork lists the cause as "asphyxia due to aspiration of stomach contents" — she had choked on her own vomit.

Hospital officials did realise that another of Diana's children had died there too. But they wrote it off as just one of those tragic coincidences in life.

Husband Lionel Garza was less easily satisfied. He had been viewing the remorseless death-roll of their babies with growing suspicion and worry. On the very morning Melissa died, he had been playing with her before he went to work. Yet half an hour after arriving there, he got a call to say his little girl was dead. Without even waiting for funeral number three, he quit home — although Diana was pregnant with their fourth child.

It was almost exactly two years later that she had a fourth

131

Deadly Diana Lumbrera - child murderer.

Top: Methodist Hospital where Jose Lionel Garza died in 1978.

Below: The grave of baby Joanna Garza - the first of seven children to die suspiciously.

JOANNA L.
GARZA
AUG 18, 1976
V 30, 1976
WE MISS THEE

child's death to announce. This time it was not one of her own. She swept into West Plains Medical Center at Muleshoe, near her home town of Bovina, carrying the body of six-week-old Ericka Aleman, whom she had been baby-sitting for her cousin Benita. Ericka was dead on arrival.

A post-mortem was ordered. But, whatever the report said, it somehow disappeared. Officials were left with the recollection that, according to Diana Lumbrera, Ericka had just "quit breathing". More attention would certainly have been paid if she had mentioned the three previous deaths.

But the toll was far from complete. On 17 August, 1982, Diana regretted to report the death, at home, of her two-year-old daughter Melinda. A pathologist ruled out crime. He decided she had heart disease and died of "acute heart failure".

Diana, by now divorced and using her maiden name Lumbrera again, took Jose Alvonis as a lover. On 10 October, 1983, she gave birth to his son, Christopher. Just short of six months later, on 28 March, 1984, his mother carried him into West Plains Memorial Hospital at Dimmitt, near Bovina. The story, this time supported by Diana's aunt Maria Aleman and sister Virginia Bribiesca, was that little Christopher turned purple while being fed.

Dr Brian Lee diagnosed septicaemia, a fatal blood infection. "There were no signs of foul play. Infants can get infections and die very quickly. They're very susceptible to them . . . the only other action I could have taken would have involved a post-mortem. But there is no pathologist at West Plains."

By now, Diana was getting rather too well known at hospitals in her own area. And the headstones of her five dead children stood side by side in the Bovina Cemetery. So in 1985 she moved over the state border, to Garden City. Soon afterwards she gave birth to her sixth child, Jose Antonio, another Alvonis baby. Considering whom he had for a mother, this second Jose lasted a comparatively long time. But after four years, on 1 May, 1990, he died.

After the post-mortem, Bovina Police Chief Gary Coleman investigated the deaths. And Lumbrera was charged with Jose Antonio's murder. She claimed she had been cursed by a "curandero" — a witch. Her friend Maria Antillon said, "She used to tell me her mother-in-law had cursed her."

At her trial, District Attorney Ricklin Pierce claimed that she murdered Jose Antonio for three reasons: she'd inherit a lump sum if her son died, she was heavily in debt — and she was psychologically disturbed.

Diana wanted to collect on a $3,000 insurance policy, he said, just as she had done with her three daughters. In answer to this, defence lawyer Mike Quint pointed out that $2,000 went on Jose's funeral. The prosecutor suggested that she probably planned the funeral when Jose was born — and only needed to make a small profit.

The second motive alleged was that Diana, up to her eyes in debt, needed to cut down on expenses. She had to shell out $25 a week, for instance, to a childminder while she worked at a meat-packing warehouse. Lastly, he claimed, Diana was a "sympathy junkie". The jury heard of a mind disease called Munchausen's Syndrome, which drives people to fake illnesses to gain sympathy. In this case she did it "by proxy", killing her son so that she could star as the grieving mother.

Diana had also lied to friends to gain their sympathy. She told them her father had died in a car crash and that Jose had leukaemia and she needed money for his chemotherapy.

Although the jury were not told of the other deaths, they convicted her of killing Jose. She was jailed for life. Under a plea-bargaining arrangement in Texas, to save taxpayers' money on a lengthy trial, she admitted killing three more of her children and was given further life sentences.

In Bovina, police chief Coleman is still baffled. "I can't understand why people weren't suspicious."

25

Candid Camera Killers

A Christmas party video is meant to be a happy memento of the festive season. For one family, a home movie brings back only memories of horror.

In front of a twinkling Christmas tree a man brandishes a gift-wrapped package and flashes a toothy smile for the video camera. A highly seasonal home movie. Until you look closer – and see the gun peeping out of its holster at his waist.

The movie was shot while two murderous thieves waited for their victims to arrive at a three-storey holiday cabin in the snowbound hills near Salt Lake City, Utah. The man with the gift was Von Lester Taylor, 26. Behind the camera was his accomplice, Edward Deli, 22. Both were petty crooks on parole. The prey they lay in wait for, three days before Christmas 1990, was the Tiede family from Humble, Texas. They were rich businessman Rolf Tiede, 50; his wife, Kaye, 49; daughters Linea, 20, and Trisha, 16, and Mrs Kaye's handicapped, partly-blind mother, Mrs Beth Botts, 72.

Rolf Tiede had taken the family Christmas to Salt Lake City. Overnight, the killers moved in. They helped themselves to drinks, tried on Rolf's clothes and opened presents.

Kaye Tiede, her mother, and her daughter Linea were first back. They were ambushed by Taylor, who had a .38 calibre pistol, and Deli with a long-barrel .44 hand gun. The pair demanded cash. "We'll give you the money!" Kaye cried. "Anything!"

But, as the women pleaded for their lives, the robbers started shooting. Blood sprayed everywhere. Kaye Tiede was

Top: Rolf Tiede with wife, Kaye and their daughters who were kidnapped.

Above: Accomplice Edward Deli.

hit once in the back with the .44 and twice in the neck with the .38. Her mother was shot once in the head, twice in the chest.

Daughter Linea sobbed and prayed. "That's not going to work," Taylor sneered. "I'm a Devil worshipper." She was tied, gagged and thrown into a cupboard. Hours later, her father and Trisha returned.

They too were ambushed, this time in the garage. Rolf handed over all his money. "Not enough," said Taylor. He ordered Deli to shoot Rolf. Deli didn't fire. So Taylor did it. But the blast didn't kill him. He played dead.

The killers decided to burn the house. They poured petrol around — and all over Rolf, who moved slightly. They noticed . and Taylor fired into Rolf's head. Yet still he did not die.

Taylor and Deli rounded up the two girls, set light to the petrol and fled in two of the snowmobiles with their captives. Once they had gone, Rolf struggled to his feet and stumbled around, looking in vain for his wife and mother-in-law. He stamped on the flames — and became a ball of fire.

Blinded by blood, seared by flames, he ripped off most of his clothes and staggered out of the blazing building, into the freezing cold. He drove the second snowmobile two miles to where his brother Randy waited to be picked up, to join the family for Christmas.

Randy hardly recognised bleeding, blistered Rolf. He called the police by car phone and within minutes, the killers' vehicle was spotted. They were off the road and were arrested. Mercifully, the two sisters weren't hurt.

In court at Coalville, Taylor admitted first-degree murder. He was sentenced to die by firing squad or poison injection. Deli denied both murders and blamed Taylor for all the shooting. One juror held out for second-degree murder, with no death penalty, so Deli got life.

Rolf Tiede, despite the horror, has had the cabin rebuilt. "I just think of Taylor and Deli as animals, stalking their prey. They were without emotion, other than feelings of cruelty. But there's no sense dwelling on it. We're going to enjoy the cabin, I'll hear my wife's laughter there again and know she's watching us.''

Will they gather at the cabin this Christmas? "No," says Rolf. "Not for Christmas. Not ever again."

26

I Was an Undercover Lover

Brunette beauty Kim Paris finally found herself the perfect job. She quit her spot as a topless go-go dancer at Caligula One to work two doors up the street at the Clyde Wilson private detective agency. As an undercover private eye, every day was riddled with danger. But the 29-year-old from Houston, Texas, had no idea it would mean she'd have to become a cold-blooded killer's lover.

Kim's very first assignment as a super-sleuth meant she had to go back to taking off her clothes – this time at a nudist club in California.

"It took me four days before I finally took off all my clothes," says Kim. "I was so embarrassed. It wasn't like topless dancing at a bar where you cannot see the customers' faces because of the bright lights." She was on the trail of a young mother at the centre of a child custody case and her evidence helped the husband win the tug-of-love battle.

She also worked on suspected insurance scams, proving that "invalid" employees really were healthy enough to work. Curvy Kim would ring claimants' doorbells and ask for help changing the tyre of her car. Few men could resist the beautiful damsel in distress and as they set to work, a hidden camera took pictures which led to charges of fraud.

But it was the way she helped crack the mysterious murder of a wealthy couple that turned her into a local hero. It was this startling story that was turned into a movie – *Love and Lies*, soon out on video in Britain. And plans are under way for a Hollywood TV series based on Kim's daring exploits.

It all began a couple of years before Kim joined the detective agency in 1984. Two masked intruders burst in on millionaire attorney James Campbell, 55, and his wife Virginia, 50, as they lay in bed, and shot them dead. Their grandchildren, Michael, eight, and Matthew, seven — who'd been lying in sleeping bags at the foot of their bed — were woken by gunfire and found themselves splattered in their grandparents' blood.

Among those interviewed by the police were the murdered victims' daughter Cynthia Ray, 35, and her boyfriend David West, 34. And suspicions were aroused immediately when they gave each other perfect alibis. Her three sisters also suspected Cynthia because she'd once boasted that she was going to kill her parents for their money. The dishy divorcee, who had given her two kids to her parents to bring up, bragged to a friend she'd killed them. But the police had no proof.

For three years the chilling case went unsolved, until it was time to divide the inheritance. Then one of the sisters, Betty Hinds, turned to the Clyde Wilson detective agency in a last- ditch attempt to stop Cynthia getting a penny from the will.

After the killings, Cynthia soon dumped her partner in crime David West, and the plan was for Kim to become his undercover lover and charm the true story out of him.

"I knocked on his door and pretended I had the wrong address and asked to use the phone," explains Kim, who changed her name to Theresa while on the assignment. "David was out when I called but his friend invited me in and then asked me to go for a drink. When David joined us at the bar he didn't suspect a thing. He struck me as a gentle, chivalrous man, so it was quite easy for me to forget I was working.

"He asked me out and on our first date I knew I was on to something when he told me that he was going to open a business as an old girlfriend was coming into some money. He told me that both her parents had died in a car crash and the estate was about to be settled."

By the third date West was so infatuated with Kim that

141

he asked her to marry him. She naturally turned him down, but to try and get him to open up she said she was only interested in macho men.

He quickly admitted that he'd done some shameful things but he wouldn't say what. For 10 weeks Kim kept up the charade, seeing West five days a week and speaking to him every day on the phone. "Although we were together constantly, I never slept with him or even kissed him," says Kim. "There were times when he tried to kiss me and I'd pull away, but he was content to be close to me whatever the conditions. If we'd had sex I would have been dirty in his mind and that's not what he wanted. He was starting a new life and he wanted to forget his past. He worshipped me and it didn't matter that I wouldn't go to bed. And I really did enjoy his company — he was smart and he made me laugh.

"David was preoccupied with Cynthia. Always talking about their sex life. She would lay in bed and call him Daddy. She convinced him that her father had raped her when she was a child. He finally admitted he was hiding something about his life with Cynthia but it was 'perfectly legal'.

"I worked on persuading him he could trust me. When I felt he was ready to crack, my boss and I went to the police." After police "wired" her with a hidden microphone in her purse, Cynthia embarked on the most frightening 48 hours of her life. As she sat in the car with the callous killer, police listened from a van around the corner.

Kim told West she'd sleep with him and wanted to marry him and have children. But only if he was completely honest. This was enough to get David to confess all . . .

David said, "All right, I killed both of her parents. Cynthia begged me to do it, and I wanted to do it, frankly. And she offered me a lot of money and I said great. And the thing was that I made her stand there with me when I did it. I didn't have the belly for it. I made her go in there with me and stand right by the bed as I shot each of them three times. I didn't do anything wrong as far as I'm concerned.''

Kim was devastated at West's confession to the callous killings. ''I wanted to clap my hand over his mouth and scream, 'God, please don't tell me! You just don't know what you're doing to yourself.' ''

She was forced to see him again the following night because the police wanted enough evidence for Cynthia and David to get the death penalty.

''I was terrified, I thought he was going to kill me because now I knew about the murders.''

But the unsuspecting West was more concerned about Kim than himself when he was arrested. He only found out how he'd been set up a few days later when it was revealed on the news.

''After his arrest I was shown 40 slides of his brutal handiwork,'' says Kim. ''To see these photos was to experience the victims' agony.''

Deadly Dave had his sentence reduced to life imprisonment in return for giving evidence against Cynthia. She was found guilty of conspiracy to murder but could go free in four years.

Kim is now married with two kids. And although now working as a radio reporter, she still moonlights as an undercover private eye. ''The danger is just like a drug,'' Kim smiles.

27

Killed by His Baby Katy

George Telemachos never knew what hit him. The gunpowder burns on his eyelids showed he was fast asleep when a bullet was pumped into his brain at point-blank range.

The blast knocked 60-year-old George's dentures out of his mouth and shattered his skull. But the killer handed the gun to one of his two accomplices and said, "If he moves, shoot him again." George's dog Cocoa, who usually barked at strangers, had not warned him of the danger. Not even a growl. After checking his pulse to make sure he was dead, the killers ransacked his home. Before they fled, they stole £400 and a Movado watch.

George's friends thought he was lucky to die instantly. For if he'd survived and found out who had masterminded his murder, life wouldn't have been worth living.

A wealthy former restaurant owner, the lonely divorcee had bought a tobacco shop rather than spend time alone in his comfortable house in Fort Lauderdale, Florida. The only person who meant anything to him was daughter Katy, 19. He'd always spoiled her because she'd been born with a liver disease. The doting dad feared she would die young like her brother Tony, who succumbed to the same disease when he was five. At 10, Katy's liver started to fail as well and she had to have an emergency transplant operation. But 10 months later her body rejected the organ and she needed a second liver swap, which was successful. Her father paid medical bills totalling £30,000 out of his own pocket because her illness was not covered by his health insurance.

Over the years Telemachos had been such a devoted dad to Katy, he had little love left over for his wife Mary, and they divorced. He was devastated when, at 17, Katy had to fight for life again after her kidneys gave out. Katy's mother donated one of her kidneys.

While Katy was sick, George, a hard-working Romanian immigrant, brought her dinner from a different restaurant every night so she would not have to eat bland hospital food. The day she was released from hospital he bought her a new, red Ford Probe sports car worth £10,000. And for her 18th birthday he splashed out on a gold necklace. He also gave her the master bedroom at home so she'd have enough room for her clothes and the stuffed animals he'd given her. George bought her a cellular phone and beeper so he could contact her at any time.

She was a little rich girl who had everything. Katy's friend Caroline Hesford said, "Spoiled! She got everything she wanted."

After her second organ transplant, however, Katy began to change. And, with the change, her life began to go to pieces. She shaved the right side of her head and combed her ringlets to the left. She had two abortions and took drugs. She even smoked hash in her dad's shop. Katy, who thought George was a millionaire, started borrowing large amounts of cash from him and was seen carrying a small gun in her handbag. She was also known to keep a .38 calibre gun in her car, and told friends she was acting as "middleman" in drug deals between New York and Miami. In her diary she talked about "shipments" and "Ks" — referring to kilos of cocaine. She also wrote a mysterious note saying: "Get Danny to kill David C."

While working in her dad's shop in the spring of 1990, Katy met stocky Puerto Rican Erik Delvalle, 24, who'd dropped out of school to be a construction worker. Soon they were madly in love. But she was from an affluent suburb with everything daddy could afford to buy her, while he was a small-time drug-dealer from a very poor area of town.

Nevertheless, within weeks, Erik had given her his

grandmother's ring and asked her to marry him. And she'd said yes. But her furious father called Erik "a blue-collar worker" who was not good enough for his daughter. He also said Erik was a "walking drug attack".

George grew more concerned when money went missing from his shop — up to £350 a time. After it had happened several times, he had to face the truth — his little princess was robbing him blind.

He confronted Katy and her fiancé and screamed at them, "Get out and don't come back!" He took away her shop and house keys. So Katy and Erik leased an apartment and rented a yellow van to move their stuff, enlisting the help of his friend Vinnie Magona, 21.

Katy now hated her father so much for interfering in her life that she and Erik plotted to kill him and live on her inheritance. Erik even boasted to a friend, Cheryl Lamb, 19, about the plan, saying, "Katy, Vinnie and I are going to kill her dad. She's going to be coming into a lot of money and we'll be set for life."

Katy had calculated that her dad was worth about £3 million but the true figure was only about £200,000. And they might have got away with their callous plan if it had not been for eagle-eyed cop John Posson.

On the night of 21 July, 1990, he was patrolling in Cooper City when he spotted a yellow unlocked van with the licence plate covered up. In it he found three cold bottles of Budweiser beer, a latex surgeon's glove, a woman's wallet containing several credit cards and a driver's licence belonging to Katy. Suspecting something was going on, Posson pulled his car into the shadows and waited. A few minutes later, three figures came running down the road towards the van.

Katy, Delvalle and Magona said they had been visiting a friend on the next street. The officer was still suspicious but let them go after taking their names and addresses. When a neighbour found George's body next day, the police knew where to go. Magona broke down after 20 minutes of questioning, admitting that Delvalle "went over to the bed, told me to look outside then shot him."

He said Delvalle had offered him £200 to come along as a lookout. Magona admitted, "I said okay. I guess it was peer pressure." He also said it was Katy's job to keep the dog quiet.

Delvalle broke down and confessed after five hours at the police station. He admitted carrying the gun but insisted Katy pulled the trigger. But police discovered that after the murder he'd bragged to Cheryl Lamb that he'd pulled the trigger.

While in prison Delvalle wrote to Katy saying he still loved her. "We are not over and we will never be," it said. "We have the rest of our lives to be together. We just got to wait it out."

He also used the letters to discuss an alibi with Katy, unaware that they would be examined and used in evidence against him. Delvalle and Magona pleaded guilty to murder charges but Katy denied it.

At her trial, Delvalle had a change of heart and said he shot George to stop him wrecking his marriage plans. "Katy reacted badly when I told her I'd killed her dad," he said. "I pleaded with her not to say anything."

Delvalle testified that after drinking a few beers and smoking some pot, he and Magona sneaked into the Telemachos house and shot George in bed. Proclaiming her innocence, Katy supported her fiancé's statement and said she knew nothing about the murder plan.

"I always loved my father," she said. "I knew everything he did was for me. I couldn't believe Delvalle was so much in love with me that he could take my father away."

And she said she didn't need her dad's money. "If I wanted more money during the week, my father would give me whatever I wanted." But the prosecutor claimed Delvalle was so much in love with Katy he was willing to lie for her.

Magona testified that Katy had masterminded the murder,

and the jury were convinced she was involved. Her gun was used and police found .38 calibre hollow-point bullets, the type that had killed George, in her car.

Katy was found guilty of murder and will serve the rest of her life in jail. Delvalle was sentenced to life, with parole possible after 25 years, while Magona got four years.

28

The Hiss of Death

Wayne Pope, 38, got a gruesome idea for a murder — and it involved an unusual weapon. Cruel Wayne wanted to get rid of his adoptive mum with a lethal snakebite. And the sweet-natured old lady knew nothing about the evil thoughts of the son she had brought up as her own.

Wayne first hatched his plan when he got chatting to a stranger, Keith Davis, in a restaurant in Pensacola, Florida. Davis told Pope that his hobby was hunting snakes, and instantly Pope, who had by then been mulling over the idea of murdering his mother for three years, dreamed up the venomous plot. "You're just the man I'm looking for," he told David. And, although he didn't explain his deadly mission, he showed a keen interest in the poisonous reptiles. The following day his motive became horribly clear. Pope explained to Davis that he'd been thinking of "getting rid" of someone. He later offered David $150 to kill Kathleen Etheridge with a deadly rattlesnake. This would be followed by more money once his ill-gotten inheritance came through.

But Pope had picked the wrong man. Keith Davis went straight to the police. "I knew if I didn't go through with it, he'd just get someone else," he said. "His mother's life was in danger."

Davis was used as a stooge by the cops so they could catch Pope red-handed. They gave him a killer four-foot rattlesnake, which Davis told Pope he would use on his mother. "I agreed to hold the snake while it bit her in the neck twice and in the arms a couple of times."

Kathleen, meanwhile, was totally unaware of her son's lethal plot. He had always been a well-behaved, loving child,

149

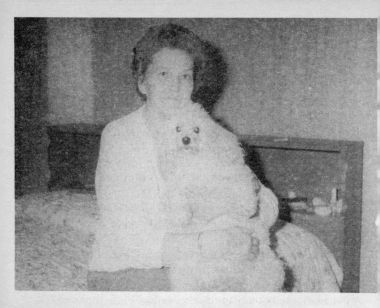

Top: Kathleen Etheridge misses the son who plotted to kill her. 'Since I lost Wayne, all I have is my dog'.

Above: Wayne Pope moved back home to mum after his marriage broke up - but her reward for welcoming him was an attempt on her life with deadly venom.

who doted on his grey-haired mum. "He was always so polite," she says. "He brought a lot of sunshine into my life."

But Pope couldn't hold down a job and had turned to petty crime to support his ex-wife and two kids. So when police called to see Kathleen, she thought he was in the usual sort of trouble. "What has Wayne done now?" she asked. The cops had to break the news of his wicked plan to astounded Kathleen.

"My heart was broken, it was very shocking," said Kathleen, who had adopted Wayne when she was with her first husband Clifford, now dead. The couple couldn't have children of their own and they took in Wayne when he was seven.

"He used to call every weekend to see how I was doing and he'd say 'I love you dearly'. But he'd got behind with his bills. I suppose he wanted my little house and car, and what I inherited on my mother's death. This is the payback I get for 30 years."

Pope wanted Davis to hold the snake so it bit the artery in her neck several times while she took her afternoon nap. Then Pope would drag the body outside to make it look like the old lady had disturbed a snake resting in her garden.

But the cops were waiting when he and Davis arrived with the snake in a sack. "He never said a word," said Kathleen. "But I'll never forget the expression on his face. He didn't even look human."

District Attorney Wade Drinkard called Pope "a sick individual", and the jury took less than 10 minutes to convict Pope of conspiracy to murder. He was sentenced to 30 years behind bars, but could get out in 10.

His mother still has forgiveness for the son she loved as her own.

"I still love and care for him," she says. "I had a miserable Christmas without him. I was always used to having him home — the first few days after his arrest I'd listen for him to come in, just like he always did."

29

The Good Twins Who Turned Evil

Which twin is the evil one? That is what heartbroken mum Robbie Good is desperate to know. Then one of her baby-faced identical twin sons, Craig and Timmy, can be cleared of a gruesome double murder. They were just 15 years old when their father William and grandmother Cleo were shot dead at point-blank range in their trailer home at Lake Murray on Saluda Island, South Carolina.

During their trial the boys blamed each other for pulling the trigger of the .22 calibre rifle. The jury took four hours to find them both guilty of the brutal slaughter.

Now their cancer-stricken mother is praying that her dying wish will be fulfilled. She wants one of them to admit he committed the murder single-handed, so an innocent twin can go free and be by her side for her last days. And she has her suspicions as to who the bad twin is.

"I love them both," wept Mrs Good. "But I honestly don't think Timmy did it. I'm convinced it was Craig who shot them. He once told me he might as well tell the truth and get it over with. But he won't own up because he wants his brother in jail to keep him company."

She believes Craig lied to the police: "He says he was out feeding the dog and Timmy says he was shaking the rug when it happened. But I've always known whether they're telling the truth or not."

The ordeal has left Robbie, 37 — she is undergoing chemotherapy for her life-threatening cancer — a physical and emotional wreck. "I can't sleep or eat anything. I have nightmares. I keep on seeing them in prison. Jail is not for children," said the distraught mother. "I think one of them was robbing my ex-husband and the gun went off," she explained. "I don't think they meant to hurt anyone."

Pranks have been part and parcel of the twins' lives, says the mum, who lost custody of her twins after a bitter divorce. Afterwards her husband had gone on the run from a drug charge and she had not seen or heard from her boys in years. She did not even know where they lived until she read the headlines about their arrest. The Good boys had been double trouble ever since they were born on 23 April, 1973. They shared the same tiny bedroom and did everything together, from doing homework to doing drugs. They were so similar they even appeared to share a psychic connection. A close relative, Anne Jones, said: "They could look at each other and instinctively know what the other was thinking."

They would swap classrooms and pretend to be each other to confuse the teachers. But their shared fun and games eventually turned to the headier and finally deadly thrills of sex, booze and drugs.

By the time they were nine, they were already selling dope for their dad. Craig's lawyer Steve McCormack blamed their poor upbringing for their lack of discipline.

"Their father let them do whatever they wanted," he said. "If they wanted to go out at night, they went out at night. He knew they did drugs and drank alcohol. He didn't care. If they didn't want to go to school, they didn't have to. In fact, he pulled them out of school so they could help him build their house."

In one year Craig missed 46 days from Irmo Middle School, while his twin missed 27 days. "Me and my dad had an arrangement," said Timmy. "I done what I wanted and he done what he wanted to." Even when the twins did manage to get to school, they were often suspended for smoking reefers, setting off the fire alarm or getting into fights.

Neighbour Dale Hewlett recalled, "There were occasions when the boys got out of control. Their father was more like a friend to the boys than a disciplinarian."

Top: Unrepentant Timmy and Craig Good return to their home town after being arrested for their horrifying murders.

Below: Robbie Good hugs Timmy and Craig before the opening of the murder trial.

He added that William, a 36-year-old electrician, had given his sons rifles for Christmas just before he was killed. The twins ran around with such a bad crowd that one official was prompted to say William and Cleo died so the boys could "party with their drug-smoking, school-cutting, beer-drinking friends".

The day after the horrific murders, schoolgirl Jill Tucker played truant to spend the day with Timmy, smoking pot and having sex, while teenager Tim Scott sold Cleo Good's rings – pocketing most of the money.

William Good and his 60-year-old mother, Cleo, whose wedding and other rings had been ripped from her fingers and stolen along with her chequebook and pick-up truck, were murdered on 20 February, 1989. But it was five days before the bodies were discovered by a neighbour who had become concerned about their Doberman pinscher moping around.

At first police thought a psycho killer was on the loose and scoured the nearby woods, expecting to find the bodies of Craig and Timmy. However, to their horror, they soon realised that the Good boys had joined forces with evil and a nationwide hunt was launched. Three days later they were arrested in their grandma's van, near their mum's home in Nashville, Tennessee.

They were broke and had been living in a cavity above the foundations of the laundry room of an apartment building. Both were high on drugs and were charged with possession. They had sold off Grandma's jewellery, paid a friend to forge her signature on $500 worth of cheques and had then gone on a drugs spree.

Craig told cops: "Most of the money we got we used to buy drugs. We stayed high all the time until we were arrested."

The twins were tried as adults. To find them guilty, jurors had to believe that both were actively involved in the decision to kill or in the killing itself.

Craig had a juvenile record including drug possession and

burgling his grandma's home. But the jury could not be allowed to hear that evidence unless he took the witness stand. He refused to testify but in a 47-page statement claimed he'd seen his father and grandmother "fall" but hadn't seen Timmy pull the trigger. Craig's lawyer told the court his client was guilty of nothing more than "looking for his brother".

However, Timmy, who'd also been busted on an earlier drug rap, testified that his twin fired the fatal shots. Although his lawyer admitted Timmy was an accessory after the fact, he added, "I think the only other thing Timmy is guilty of is not turning his brother in."

But District Attorney Don Myers, holding the murder weapon that had been covered in both boys' fingerprints, said: "It doesn't make any difference whatsoever which one pulls this trigger. They're both guilty. When two people conspire and aid and abet each other, it's just like both hands being on that trigger."

Myers later revealed that detectives on the case have changed their minds several times about who was the lesser of the two evil twins. "But it doesn't matter who did it. Our position is that it was two people with one mind — one purpose."

The bad Good boys confessed that on the day of the murders they had both been drinking stolen alcohol. Craig also passed the time by shooting holes in the trailer skylight while waiting for their dad and grandma to return to be murdered.

For four hours the jury struggled with the possibility that one of the boys did the killing while the other took no part. In the end they found both equally guilty of murder.

When the verdict was announced, Craig screamed defiantly at TV cameras, "I'll be back!" while Timmy shouted "I'm innocent". Their mother broke down and had to be half-carried, sobbing, from the courthouse.

But prosecutor Myers said, "It was sickening to have to sit and listen to these twins talk casually about the murders as if they were nothing. They think this is a big joke and they have absolutely no remorse. Their only regret is having got caught.

"They thought they were something big because they cut school, only caused trouble when they did go to school and did the things that they wanted to — most of which were criminal acts. But they're only punk potheads who murdered in cold blood. Acting big just flushed their lives down the sewer. They were both destined for prison. It was just a matter of time."

And time is something Robbie Good doesn't have much of. Craig and Timmy, sentenced to life imprisonment for murder and 65 years each for armed robbery and stealing an automobile, could be paroled in 20 years. Too late for their dying mother, who is fighting to prove that one of the twins did it by himself.

"Then maybe I can have one of my boys back," she said wistfully. "But no matter what happens, and whatever they did, I'll always love them."

30

Double Trouble

John Cassidy's wife wept like a typical bereaved widow while convincing a coroner that her distraught husband had killed himself with a shotgun. But the father-of-nine haunted his wife Mary from the grave, by proving she was the one who pulled the trigger after plotting his murder with her toyboy lover.

Mary, 29, told police she was in the upstairs bedroom when she heard a gunshot and found his body on the living room couch with a shotgun next to it. He had a large hole in his head where his chin should have been. She said that on the night before he died, her despondent 33-year-old husband had talked about killing himself. He was racked with guilt because, apart from the five children he had with his wife, he had four children with his wife's sister Bonnie McKinley.

Mary's tale about her suicidal husband was confirmed by her brother Edward Hill, who had also heard him talk about ending it all on the day of his death.

"John said he put my two sisters through too much misery and hurt them, so he wanted to alleviate the pain," said Hill. "I told him, 'John, this is not going to solve any problems except to leave two women without a husband and a lover, or whatever, and kids without a father.'"

For years, John had been having an affair with 37-year-old Bonnie, who lived with them in the same house in Monongahela, Pennsylvania. They would have sex when his wife was out shopping or working at the local corner store, or he'd creep into Bonnie's bed when Mary was asleep.

His wife finally found out about the affair and knew that

her sister was having her husband's kids, but she would not leave him because of her own children. They had bitter arguments about the affair and eventually Mary split the house into two self-contained units, hoping that would stop it. The Cassidys would live in one half while Bonnie and the rest of her husband's kids had the other half. But John and Bonnie carried on with their romance in spite of the new sleeping arrangement.

The complications of having two women in his life — and in this case both sisters living at the same house — had seemingly taken their toll on him. There were even rumours around town that he had a secret second lover and that she'd had his baby.

So it came as no surprise to his friends and family that John had taken his own life. But police were not sure it was suicide because most people kill themselves with a shot through the head or mouth, not the chin.

However, coroner Farrell Jackson ruled that a tormented Cassidy had died by his own hand on 12 February 12, 1991, and police called off their investigation into a possible homicide. But two weeks later Bonnie McKinley made a shocking discovery — a tape recording proving Mary was a killer.

With Bonnie's help, Cassidy had bugged his own phone the day before he died because he thought his wife was being unfaithful, although he was not certain who with. Tragically, John never listened to the gruesome tape or he might have been able to save his own life. He might also have been amazed to discover that her lover was David Bowers, a 17-year-old student who Cassidy often went hunting and fishing with.

After a stunned Bonnie heard the recording, she called a family meeting with her brother Edward Hill, her other sister Rose Marie Smith and Rose Marie's husband Orlando.

She told them about the tape and explained that if they went to the police, Mary would probably go to jail for a very long time. After a lot of soul-searching they all agreed to do the right thing and inform the cops.

State trooper Roy Fuller played just 15 seconds of the damning 90-minute tape to Mary before she cried: "That's enough. Turn it off." Fuller said: "I asked her, 'You killed your husband, didn't you?' She dropped her head, started to cry and then slowly nodded her head."

Cassidy's body was dug up and the red-faced coroner changed the verdict on the death certificate to murder. Coroner Jackson said: "99 per cent of what Mary Cassidy told me was true except the part about who pulled the trigger. It makes you feel like a goon."

Mary was unaware that under a state law a wiretap is inadmissible evidence when it is made without the knowledge of one of the parties being taped. This would have meant that she had a good chance of getting off scot-free in a trial because the evidence against her would have been purely circumstantial.

Although Mary confessed to the brutal killing, she claimed that she did it in self-defence because she was a battered wife. She told police that when her husband fell asleep on the couch after one of his drink and drugs benders, she stared at him with a mixture of hatred and fear. Officer Fuller said: "She was thinking about all the things that had happened in the past, all the abuse, the bad experiences. I guess she'd had it with him."

"Then she got the shotgun. She knelt down beside him and thought again about her past life. She picked up the shotgun and laid the barrel on his chin. She held her hand on the trigger. She said that she thought he was going to kill her if he awoke. She was afraid. She pulled the trigger once. She screamed. The shotgun fell."

But officials said that Mary killed her husband because she was madly in love with hunky Bowers, who went to Thomas Jefferson High School. They found cards from her addressed to "Dave" and signed "Love Mary with Xs and Os". A search of his home uncovered her class ring as well as letters and cards from her. He'd also sent her a bunch of flowers and they had spent his 17th birthday by having a sizzling romp at Seven Springs Resort, not far from their homes. District Attorney John Pettit claims that her young lover had urged Mary to murder Cassidy, and without his encouragement she would have never done it.

Mary married her bearded husband in 1973 when he was 20 and she was just 16, and they began having children almost right away. The marriage quickly went downhill because he couldn't hold down a steady job and turned into a violent, two-timing alcoholic who loved to snort cocaine.

They eventually stopped having sex, and were more likely to share a bedroom with their children than each other. Although John and Mary briefly separated, they got back together for the sake of the children, but the bitter arguments continued. Police were called to their house more than once to settle their violent fights that one time ended up with Mary claiming that he almost tried to kill her.

"He had me by the throat against the wall and was going to choke me," she said. "Instead he grabbed me by the hair and he had a knife in his hand and he just cut the top of my hair off. The next day when he got up he remembered what he did, but his reasoning was, 'Well, it's better your hair than your throat.' "

But Cassidy's mother Dolores claimed her son had never beaten his wife. "There may have been verbal abuse but I never saw black and blue marks on her," she said.

"He loved his children. She asked him for a divorce and he wouldn't give her one because of the kids."

His mum also blamed Mary for not putting an end to his relationship with Bonnie. "If you love a man, you're not going to share him with another woman, especially your sister."

Mary pleaded guilty to third, degree murder charges under a plea bargain in which she'll give evidence against her lover. She faces from five to ten years in jail.

After an investigation by child welfare, her kids were

handed over to the care of her relatives. Bowers was held under house arrest for several weeks after the murder and had a teacher come to his house every day to give him lessons. But now he has gone back to school while he awaits trial early next year on charges of soliciting a murder.

31

He Bumped off his Buddies

It seemed like harmless fun — two young boys playing war games. Except that when 13-year-old Richard Bourassa invited his best friend Jeffrey Bush — also 13 — to his house to play after school on 12 September, 1986, the gun he gave him was real.

Coolly, Richard brought out two guns that belonged to his father. He gave the .22 calibre rifle to Jeff while he kept the 12-gauge shotgun. They had a mock shoot-out until eventually they stood face-to-face, aiming the two loaded guns at each other as if they were toys.

Suddenly the gun-barrels touched and the shotgun went off, spraying the room with buckshot. The pellets hit the door and window and several riddled Jeff's head and body. He died the next day.

Richard sobbed as he called the police and explained what had happened. But later he managed a sick smile — as he was photographed with arms, legs, his shorts and T-shirt covered in blood. He told the police Jeff loaded the guns himself because he didn't know how. With no witnesses, the coroner ruled that this was a case of accidental death.

Four years later, on 24 May, 1990, Richard, by now 17, called another friend, 17-year-old Christian Wiedepuhl, over to play Nintendo at his house in Anaheim Hills, California.

Incredibly, in the same room and at the same time of day — just after 4pm — more deadly gunplay took place. This time the police found Christian lying on the floor, dying from a single wound. A bullet had smashed one lens of his glasses and entered his head above his eyebrow.

Bourassa told the detectives that Christian had been

Right: Teenaged killer Richard Bourussa in custody.

Middle right: Weedy Christian Wiedepuhl saw Richard as his protector and pal until the moment the 'minder' let loose with the shotgun.

Below left: Cool killer Richard sits smiling, covered in the blood of his pal.

Below right: Jeff Bush, 13, was riddled with pellets - the first to be killed by the teenager's deadly game with guns.

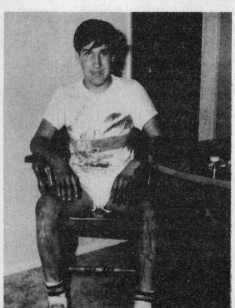

searching through the house and had discovered a .38 Smith & Wesson revolver in the headboard of his stepfather's bed. He had then pointed the weapon at Richard's head.

"I told him to give me the gun," said Bourassa. "Then he told me it wasn't loaded. But I asked him again to give me the gun. He handed it to me and then looked down to get the holster. And that's when it went off. There was a loud explosion and my ears were ringing."

He claimed Christian had loaded the gun, as he knew little about firearms. Asked why he'd had his finger on the trigger, he replied, "I don't know — I have no idea."

Bourassa's story of the shooting had a chillingly familiar ring to it, coming after the one he told four years earlier. It was left to the police to decide whether he was a cold-blooded killer or just a victim of hideous bad luck. After an intense four-month investigation, they charged Bourassa with murder.

When Christian's parents learned that Richard had killed before, they were horrified. "If I had known," said his heartbroken father, Ricky Wiedepuhl, "then I wouldn't have allowed my son to go to Richard's house."

For four years Jeff Bush's father, Dale, had believed his son's death was a tragic accident. But when he heard of Christian's killing, he changed his mind.

"Richard is sick. How many deaths will it take to show he's a killer?" he said.

Forensic tests did show that the lack of gunpowder on Christian's face indicated the shot that killed him wasn't fired at close range. Also, the ballistics tests stated that "no way could the trigger have fired without direct pressure".

The prosecuting lawyer, Kathy Harper, claimed that Richard had found the gun, which his dad had left loaded, then used Christian as target practice in a grotesque game of Russian roulette in reverse. He took out one bullet (police found it on his bed), then fired at Christian to scare him. Richard had then expected the empty chamber would come up next. But he had miscalculated the direction in which the barrel would rotate. He fired the gun and killed Christian.

This constituted murder under Californian law because of his wilful disregard for life. The prosecutor also claimed the murder was premeditated. "The killing involved a high degree of planning," he said.

The biggest flaw in Bourassa's story was that he'd said he had no knowledge of guns. He was, in fact, fascinated by them. He'd written a project on infantry weapons at school and he also collected spent 12-gauge shotgun shells.

"Richard liked to take the .38 out and point it at people to scare them," said Kathy Harper. "He liked to load it and pretend to shoot at people. Enemies, burglars – even friends."

Three of Bourassa's friends also testified that he had pointed guns at them in the past, including the shotgun that blasted Jeff Bush. A close friend, Tony Cordova, revealed that Richard had twice brought out the deadly .38 while he was over at Bourassa's house, and he'd removed the bullets.

"Sometimes he pointed the gun at the wall," said Tony. "A few times he pointed it at my head. He'd say: 'Do you trust me? Do you trust me?' Then he'd go 'Boom!' "

"He was fooling around but I was very, very scared and it caused a rift in our friendship. I thought it was weird. I used to be over at his house every day after school – I still can't get over thinking that it could have been me he'd shot."

Another school pal, Jesse Jobe, recalled a shock he got when he was first invited to Richard's house soon after the first killing. "He was showing me all the bloodstains. I don't know if he was proud of them, but he didn't seem very bothered about blowing his best friend away."

Richard's love of firearms was picked up from his stepfather, Thomas Baldwin, a 51-year-old pilot. Baldwin was so attached to his shotgun and rifle that he still kept them even after Jeff's death – claiming he needed them for his "own protection".

Christian's father, Ricky, blamed Baldwin and Richard's

mother, Nancy, for the killing as much as he blamed the boy himself. "It was negligence," said Ricky. "A cheap gun lock would have prevented a killing. They'd already had one death and that should have been enough for them to have learnt a lesson. They shouldn't have kept those guns, but at least they could've kept them locked up.

"My son was so full of life. I'm still trying to come to terms with his death. Nothing can bring him back, and I don't want revenge, but I hope this makes people more responsible with their weapons, especially if they have kids of their own."

The investigation into Bourassa's past uncovered a troubled, trigger-happy child obsessed with death, guns, wrestling and the army. Diagnosed as dyslexic — word-blind — at the age of seven, he was a year behind at school and was often in trouble. When he was only nine, Richard's father, 39, died of a heart attack. The young boy was heart-broken as he'd idolised his dad, who helped design the military Apache helicopter.

Richard's greatest ambition was to join the army like his sister and brother-in-law. He said he wanted to become a soldier, so as to "get paid to shoot people".

Richard, just 13 when he first killed, had grown up into a 5ft 10in, 14-stone hulk by the second shooting. He jogged regularly and also pumped iron daily to train for his favourite sport, wrestling, at which he excelled. In his room he had trophies and photos of himself in the school team.

In sharp contrast Christian was six feet tall but weighed just eight stone and was considered a wimp by his classmates at Canyon High School. But they backed off teasing him when Bourassa became his friend and personal bodyguard. Ironically, after giving him the protection he needed, it was Richard who went on to kill his schoolmate.

Bourassa's lawyer, Edward Hall, claimed it was all a horrific coincidence, but added, "A lot of people feel he must never have access to guns again."

The day before the trial was due to start, Richard shocked

his lawyer by pleading guilty to second-degree murder. He admitted "knowingly" pointing the gun at Christian.

Hall was "flabbergasted". He had expected his client to serve a short sentence for manslaughter. But this surprise murder plea suddenly opened the way to a much heavier penalty — 15 years to life.

32

The Tragic Tale of
Derrick Jones and Amy Smith

Teenagers Derrick Jones and Amy Smith were like a modern-day *Romeo and Juliet*. Because he was black and she was white, their undying love for each faced an uphill struggle from the start. Both sets of parents were dead set against the romance. Her father Dennis – a policeman for 20 years – did not want to meet her boyfriend and refused to have him in the house. But Amy, 16, and Derrick, 17, continued to secretly see each other. And, just like Shakespeare's teens, their relationship ended in heartbreaking tragedy.

Her father shot Derrick dead after finding him inside his home in the middle of the night. Derrick's family claimed their son had been gunned down in anger when Smith caught his daughter with a black man.

But Dennis Smith was never charged with murder. Instead there was an incredible twist in the case that stunned conservative politicians in nearby Washington, DC.

The tragic tale began at 3am on 3 July, 1991, when Smith and his wife Mariaelena say they woke up to find an intruder in their bedroom. The six-foot burglar, wearing rubber gloves and a ski mask, stood over the bed in the dark holding a gun, handcuffs and a kitchen knife. He gave the handcuffs to Dennis, 46, and ordered him to put them on. After Smith handcuffed one of his wrists, the intruder clamped the other cuff to the bedpost.

Then the gunman walked around the bed towards a naked Mariaelena, waved the gun at her husband and shouted: "I have no problem killing a cop!" After telling her to lie on the bed and stay put, he left the room to grab silverware

169

and $357 in cash. He came back three times to check the Smiths had not moved.

At one point he found the keys to Mariaelena's car and said to her: "I got your car — what are you going to do now?"

Mrs Smith told police: "I told him I didn't care. It was like I wasn't afraid of him any more. I knew I was going to die. I didn't care."

She was more concerned for her stepdaughter's safety in the next room. "I was scared he was going to hurt her." Her fears were ironic in the light of what would happen later. After he'd finished looting the house, the gunman handed the knife to Mariaelena and ordered her to stab her husband to death.

She recalled: "At this point I asked God to forgive my sins and to receive me now." When he again told her to stab Dennis, she said: "No way."

It was at this point that Smith — who had loosely handcuffed his wrist — broke free from his cuffs and charged the intruder.

Smith wrestled with him in the bedroom and down the hallway while screaming at his wife — who still had the knife — to "stab him, stab him". But she was unable to bring herself to do it.

The cop and the burglar ended up struggling in the bathroom, where Smith pushed him in the tub. As he fell backwards, the thief dropped the weapon. While Mrs Smith was picking up the gun and handing it to her husband, the burglar sprang up and ran downstairs to the front door.

Instead of running out, he ran back up the stairs and charged towards Smith. The officer shot him once in the chest and once in the head. Smith pulled off the mask. The man was black and Smith had never seen him before.

Meanwhile, a terrified Amy had heard the struggle and called the police. The operator said to her: "What's the problem, ma'am?"

170

Amy replied: "We have a prowler in the house and he's trying to kill my parents."

The operator said: "Does he have a gun?"

She said: "No, I mean yes."

Then there was a popping noise in the background. "What was that?" asked the operator.

Amy: "That was my dad's gun."

After she hung up, she ran out to see if her parents were alive. When she saw the intruder lying on the floor, covered in blood, she broke down and wept.

Her father comforted his hysterical daughter until the police arrived at their four-bedroom house in Prince George's County, Maryland, a middle-class suburb of Washington. What looked at first like a simple robbery to the cops turned into a shocking case of attempted murder most foul.

Detectives found a front door key in the burglar's pockets, and in a shopping bag left by the front door they found a sketch of the inside of the house.

The map showed where Smith kept his handcuffs and 9mm semi-automatic service pistol, which the burglar had been using. And it showed the kitchen where he got the knife.

It was not long before police learned the intruder's identity – Derrick Jones, who had been going out with Amy for just three months. And police soon found that it was Amy's handwriting on the map. Police also uncovered several handwritten notes between the lovers in which Amy told Derrick to shoot her in the shoulder before leaving the house.

Police arrested Amy, a student at Friendly High School, and charged her as an adult with attempted murder and conspiracy to commit murder. They said she was supposed to survive a robbery during which her parents were to be killed.

Her father said that when he and his wife were told Amy had been arrested for trying to kill them, "We almost fell right out of our chairs. We were stunned. It was unbelievable, unreal."

The Smiths refused to pay £25,000 to bail her out of jail because they were afraid that she might try to kill them again if she lived in their home. Brunette Amy, a heavy-set girl whose mother died in a car crash when she was a baby, spent a month in a psychiatric centre before her father picked her up to return her to jail.

"You don't know what it's like, bringing your daughter to a place where you've been bringing prisoners for 20 years," said Smith. "It's the hardest thing I've ever done in my life."

But Derrick's family and friends — who live in the middle-class town of Fort Washington — believed the shooting was not self-defence but motivated by Smith's hatred of blacks. Elbert Jones, Derrick's dad, said: "The wrong person is on trial. It should be Amy's father. My son has never, never in his whole life had any contact with the police. Never in any trouble. Never."

Jones, who worked on the Washington subway system, added that Derrick went to Amy's home that night just to make love with her. "Him being a young man and her being a young woman. It was a sexual thing."

Derrick's friend Antoine Base said: "I think Smith shot Derrick because he didn't want a black man to be with his daughter."

Another friend, Greg Drew, added: "The father probably came in and saw Amy with a black guy and didn't like it so he probably shot him."

Amy, who opted for a non-jury trial in front of Judge Hovey Johnson, did not testify but claimed through her lawyer that there was no plot to rob and kill her parents.

Her attorney Elvira White alleged that her father had shot Jones in a rage after catching him in the house with his daughter. White suggested that Smith shot Jones in the head as he lay motionless on the floor and then invented the robbery story to justify the shooting.

But the prosecutor Beverly Woodard said: "This is a crime that no parent wants to believe could happen. But the evidence shows it did."

Greg Drew, who was also a friend of Amy's, testified that she had once remarked to him that she wanted her father dead. She also told Drew that her dad was "too strict" and "wouldn't let her do a lot of things". Smith especially didn't like her dating black youths.

And teenager Tony Harding told the court that Amy had tried to buy a gun a month before the shooting "so she could kill her parents". He thought she was joking at first but eventually realised she was serious.

Mariaelena's dramatic testimony of the shooting convinced the judge that there was a robbery-murder plan.

But Derrick's dad Elbert said: "Mrs Smith gave a stellar performance. She must have been directed by Steven Spielberg or somebody."

Nevertheless, it was Amy's own words that were the most damaging to her. When she called the police at the time of the shooting, she was asked: "Does he [the intruder] have a gun?"

Although she was in her bedroom, she replied: "No, I mean yes." She knew that Jones had her father's gun and that he was probably using it at that moment to kill her parents.

When the operator heard the gunshot, he asked: "What was that?" Amy replied: "That was my dad's gun." How would she know it was her dad's gun — unless she had plotted to kill him?

After a two-day trial, Judge Johnson said there was "no doubt" in his mind that Amy enlisted Jones to kill her parents and make it look like a robbery. He said Jones took a subway train and a bus to Amy's house and climbed in through a window that she had left open. After robbing the house, he was supposed to kill her parents and then escape in her stepmother's car, following Amy's directions to a nearby highway.

Johnson said: "For two teenagers to go to this length boggles the mind." After he gave his guilty verdict, one of Derrick's uncles screamed at Dennis Smith: "You're a murderer, you're a murderer, and you let your daughter take the fall."

Amy was sentenced to 15 years for planning to kill her father. But Smith stated: "We love our daughter and we have forgiven her. She's still just a child inside. When she is ready to see me, I plan to visit her in jail and be there for her when she goes free."

Derrick's family, however, is not convinced justice has been done, and they have hired a private eye to conduct their own investigation.

33

Programmed to Kill

The office needed a clearout. The man who used to work there had left in disgrace and would not be coming back. As US Marine sergeant William Kane set about the job, he noticed a computer disk on the desk.

In case it contained important information, he popped the disk into a computer and called up the list of files it contained. One was entitled Murder. Intrigued, Sgt Kane opened the file on screen. And was startled by what he read.

"How do I kill her? . . . What to do with the body? Make it look as if she left . . . Check in library on ways of murder . . ."

Last on this disturbing check-list: "Blame it on her own kind."

The man who had written that list was former Marine captain Robert Russell, aged 34. His office at Gulfport, Mississippi, was being cleared because he had been thrown out of the service for theft and drunkenness.

The Murder file could have been just some bizarre computer game. But Sgt Kane was worried. He recalled Russell once asking: "If you drop a hairdryer or TV into a bathtub, can it really kill somebody?"

When Russell was dishonourably discharged, in 1988, he had been married for just a few months to a fellow captain, 29-year-old Shirley. It was an unlikely match. Twice-married Russell was white and a loudmouthed racist. His bride was black. Which gave a special meaning to that last line on the Murder file: "Blame it on her own kind."

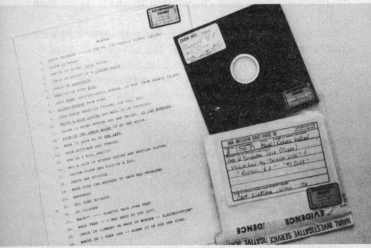

Top: The victim - 29 yr old Shirley Russell.

Below: Piecing together the jigsaw - the disc, with spelling mistakes intact, trapped Robert Russell as Shirley's murderer.

The balding Russell himself was ready enough to blame his wife's colour for his lack of promotion. He once remarked to a colleague, "I wonder what they'll think when they find out who I'm married to."

Sgt Kane was alarmed enough to report the murder disk to his commander – and to call Shirley at her new married officers' quarters in Quantico, Virginia, to warn her, "Be very careful."

But the Murder file was dismissed as some kind of computer game. And Shirley, still the new young wife, shrugged off the warning. Her disgraced husband – sharing her Marine quarters now as the civilian spouse of a serving officer – got a teaching job at North Stafford High School, in Alexandria, just on the outskirts of Washington, DC. Almost straightaway, Russell began a steamy love affair with a curvy colleague, brunette Sandy Flynt. They often used to sneak back to Russell's married quarters for lunchtime sex – on 15 occasions, Sandy later admitted. Once, wife Shirley came home unexpectedly while Sandy was dozing on the couch. The teacher escaped unseen. That night, on the phone, she and Russell joked about it.

"Close, eh?" Russell said. Sandy replied, "You're not kidding. Oh Lord, I'll know now not to fall asleep on your couch again."

"No sweat," her lover assured her.

But he was forgetting that he had bugged his own phone with a tape-recorder because, in spite of all the womanising and race-hate talk, he was desperately possessive of his wife. That exchange with Sandy was duly taped. Later on, Shirley found it.

A year after the move to Quantico, Russell began threatening to kill her. That, on top of his womanising and bigotry, was the end for Shirley. She moved in with a relative. On 4 March, 1989, she returned to clean out the place, before the next couple moved in. She was never seen again.

Russell raised the alarm. He told police and Naval

Investigative Service officers that Shirley went to buy paint at a store five miles away, and had not returned. He assumed, he said, she had deserted the Marines.

For months, the navy and FBI searched for clues, sure that Shirley had been murdered. Her husband had bought a .25 calibre gun two days before she vanished. Russell claimed he had given it to her, for her own protection.

Investigators also discovered his wife-murder threats, made to several people. He had paid a surprise visit to his parents in neighbouring Pennsylvania – a chance to agree on an alibi. And he had cleaned a store room at home with an acid known for its power to erase bloodstains.

Shirley's body was never found. But law officers decided they had enough evidence for a murder charge without it.

In court at Alexandria, the jury heard how, apart from bugging his own phone, Russell had hidden a tape-recorder under his wife's car seat – and after she walked out, even raided her relative's house and put another recorder under her bed.

Lover Sandy Flynt told of the time Russell said, "I'm going to kill her. They'll never be able to prove it. I'll blow her up and make it look like a terrorist act. Or I'll poison her."

Sandy testified, "He seemed serious. I just hoped he was joking." But, she added, she got a big shock when Russell showed her a six-inch metal tube and asked, "Have you ever seen a home-made silencer?"

Russell's lover also told how she had spent some lunch dates just helping him to follow his wife. Once, she said, while Shirley was jogging, he jumped out of his car and chased her.

The accused man's brother, Ronald, a miner, told the jury that Robert once asked him to get some dynamite, to "blow up Shirley".

Russell's first wife, Pamela, gave weight to a theory that

the body might have been cut up and dumped in rubbish bags down abandoned mineshafts. "He knew that area like the back of his hand," she said.

Shirley's mother, Annie Sumpter, said her daughter wanted to cut Russell out of a $30,000 life insurance policy, because of his many threats.

Marine lieutenant Tommy Maris dismissed the claim that Shirley had deserted. "She was a super officer," he said. "Shirley had a high degree of integrity, courage and reliability."

Defence lawyer Fred Fanelli insisted that Shirley was alive. He produced four people to say they had seen her after the alleged murder. As for the computer-disk file that the prosecution called a "Recipe for Murder", the defence claimed it was all to do with writing a novel.

Robert's loyal mum, Patricia Russell, told the jury that she and her son had been writing a book about the death of a US Marine officer's wife. "We never determined whether she was going to be killed by a gang, or by accident," she said. "I was helping with the feminine aspect of a character — where a woman would hide the jewellery, that sort of thing."

So where was the manuscript of this alleged novel? "I threw it away," Patricia explained.

The prosecutor, Lawrence Leiser, claimed that Patricia and her husband — another Robert — had lied in evidence to protect their son.

An ex-girlfriend, Doreen Evans, swore Russell had borrowed books to help write a novel. But the prosecutor suggested she was still in love with him. Leiser went through the computer's Murder list of things to do, such as "10: Write a nice letter" — a reference to a note that Russell actually left saying, "Shirley, where's the paint? I love you."

Then there was "17: Vacuum floor and tidy up a bit." Russell had done that too. He had also washed his car the day after the alleged murder.

It took the jury 16 hours to decide that Russell was a killer; he was given a life sentence.

Russell is appealing against the verdict and still insists he is innocent. But after the trial, he said, in a tell-tale slip, "I guess I'm the only one who really knows what happened."

34

The Mastermind Murderer

George Trepal is a computer wizard with a genius IQ, a member of Mensa, which puts him among America's top intellectuals — but George also has an extremely poisoned mind.

So much so that the man who loved scripting murder mystery weekends plotted a warped attack on his neighbours that left one woman dead, two teenage boys partially paralysed and four others horribly sick.

And all because the bright boffin, an avid Agatha Christie fan, has a lethal fascination with poison.

George and his wife Diana often organised murder mystery weekends for fellow members of the high-IQ Mensa society, in which the players were given a script and acted out the plot. The victims met several sticky ends — shootings, drownings, beatings and strangulations — but at least half were from poisoning, George's favourite murder most foul.

Says Ernest Prince, who took part in the crime puzzles, "If someone was going to be poisoned, George would find out what symptoms they'd get and how much it may be investigated. He was always very thorough."

But his quest for perfection didn't cross over into real life, for when George put his poisoned murder plan into action for real, he made some very simple mistakes that meant his crime didn't remain a mystery for long.

In October 1988 in Bartow, Florida, the seemingly mild-mannered Trepal, 42, struck down his next door neighbours with poisoned bottles of Coca-Cola. Peggy Carr, 41, died a slow and painful death five months after the attack. Her

Top: Pye Carr and victim Peggy Carr in 1986.

Below: Cool Killer. Even when faced with the evidence - the lethal thallium - George Trepal still denied his hideous crimes. But cop Susan Goreck says his intellect made him curious to kill, and the mad Mensa murderer had a passion for poison.

son Duane, 19, and stepson Travis, 18, were left partially paralysed. Her husband Parealyn and three others, including a two-year-old girl, luckily only suffered sickness, from which they fully recovered.

An eight-pack of 16oz Coke bottles found in their kitchen had been laced with thallium nitrate, a rare colourless, odourless poison outlawed since 1965. Just one gram of it is enough to kill a full-grown man.

The FBI was called in, but tampering at the plant was soon ruled out. Then attention turned to Trepal and his wife Diana — because they were the only possible people with a motive to harm the Carrs.

Even so, at first George Trepal was not a suspect. He was interviewed only in order to eliminate him from the enquiry. Then several clues began to point to him as the killer.

For the six years that they were neighbours, the Trepals had numerous run-ins with the Carrs. George complained they played their radio too loud and drove their jeeps over his property.

The last argument occurred on October 17, 1988 — when Diana and Peggy rowed over the Carrs' loud music blaring out. Two days later, Peggy Carr began suffering nausea and aching joints. Within a fortnight, Peggy and her sons were in hospital.

Peggy was racked with pain, her hair fell out and she clung feebly to life for only another four months. Within two months she had slipped into a coma from which she never recovered. On March 3, 1989, her family took the tragic decision to switch off the life-support system.

Three months earlier, the Carrs had received a chilling typewritten message that read: "You and all your so-called family have two weeks to move out of Florida forever or else you die. This is no joke."

When police asked George who could want his neighbours dead, he calmly replied, "Someone probably wanted them to move out." A cool response that had chilling overtones after the threatening note. Then, when the police began to look into George's past, they uncovered a stunning and hideous history.

The chemistry buff had a history of trying to poison pets and had even tried to secretly drug his flatmates at college, 20 years before. To keep them from eating his food, he smeared his doorknob and the fridge door with a hallucinatory drug. He once injected drugs, possibly amphetamines, into biscuits during a trip and handed them to unsuspecting people.

He also tried to poison his wife's dog by feeding it Valium and, whenever they rowed, he frequently threatened to poison her pet cats.

Then it was discovered that George had served two and a half years in jail in 1975 for helping to run a $4 million illegal methamphetamine (commonly known as crack) manufacturing operation. The elaborate process uses the very dangerous poison thallium nitrate. The evidence was still circumstantial, however, so undercover cop Susan Goreck, 35, was put on the case. She joined in one of George and Diana's Mensa murder weekends and befriended the couple. It soon became apparent that George was the type of person who would commit that type of poisoning murder.

"A person who might do something like this can't deal with situations directly," says Bill Hagmaier, an agent at the FBI Behavioural Science Unit in Virginia (the unit featured in the hit movie thriller *The Silence Of The Lambs*). "They deal with conflicts in a cowardly way."

Susan Goreck found George to be a charming man, interesting to be with and very amusing. But she had to be careful. "If we went out to dinner and I had to leave to go to the bathroom, I wouldn't eat anything I'd left at the table. I had to be very aware of it at all times."

In December 1989, George and Diana moved to Seabring, Florida, so that Diana, an orthopaedic surgeon, could open a new practice. They were delighted to rent their old house to their new friend. It was then that their house was thoroughly searched. Not only did police uncover a phial

184

containing thallium nitrate, but also a copy of Agatha Christie's *The Pale Horse* — a tale about a pharmacist who kills by putting thallium nitrate into food and medicine.

Those who knew George were amazed at the findings. Whodunit pal Ernest Prince says, "I find it so unbelievable. He was a great guy. He seemed so nice and friendly."

At his trial, Trepal pleaded innocent to the charges and even tried to accuse his wife of the grisly deed. But district attorney John Aguero told the jury: "This is the most diabolical man you will ever see before you in your life. What we have here is a man who thought he was so smart that he could commit the perfect crime. But he was not so smart."

In just six hours, the jury brought back guilty verdict and, as Carr family members watched in the courtroom, the judge sentenced George Trepal to die in "old sparky" — the electric chair.

Peggy's sister says she wants to be the one to turn on the electric current personally. "I believe in an eye for an eye, a tooth for a tooth," she says.

But Susan Goreck thinks Trepal killed not so much from hatred or rage but for sheer intellectual pleasure. "I think it was a game to him," she says of the man she found both extremely charming and pleasant to be with. "He really thought he had committed the perfect crime."

35

Daddy's Girl

Two-timing computer tycoon David Brown thought he'd found the perfect way to murder his wife – and he very nearly got away with it. He brainwashed his 14-year-old daughter Cinnamon into killing her stepmum Linda, so he could marry his secret mistress – his wife's teenage sister, Patti Bailey, who was also a conspirator in the murder.

Brown, a $100,000-a-year computer boss, had bombarded both girls with his evil thoughts to get rid of his 23-year-old wife Linda, mother of his seven-month-old daughter. The evil schemer persuaded them to kill for him by constantly telling them, "If you love me, you'll do it for me." Brown, who loved Agatha Christie thrillers, told them he could not do the dirty deed himself because he was a sickly person who "did not have the stomach" to kill his wife of three years.

He convinced them that Linda and her twin brother Alan had ties to the Mob and were planning to kill him and take over his growing computer business. His reasoning was so effective that Patti had even gone to her sister's bedroom one night and aimed a gun at her. But when it came to it, Patti couldn't pull the trigger. "I couldn't do it," she said. "She was my sister, I loved her."

So it was left to Cinnamon to do the dirty deed. The gruesome murder took place in the early hours of 19 March 1985, in a quiet house on a suburban street in Los Angeles. After weeks of secret plans, Brown woke Cinnamon and her stepmum's young sister Patti to say "Girls, it has to be done tonight." Cinnamon took a .38 Smith & Wesson, given to her by Brown, wrapped a towel round it and crept into Linda's bedroom. To muffle the sound of gunfire even further, she stuck it in a pillow and then shot her stepmother as she lay sleeping.

But the shot made the baby cry, and then Linda gave an awful gasp. Cinnamon screamed, "She's not dead!" and ran back in the room and pumped another shot into her.

The second silver-tipped bullet in the chest was enough to kill her. Cinnamon quickly scribbled the suicide note which Brown had made her practise countless times before. "Dear God, please forgive me," it said. "I didn't mean to hurt her."

It was meant to look like a murder, followed by attempted suicide. Cinnamon would swallow a "safe" dose of pills – she firmly believed she wouldn't die from taking the tablets her loving dad had given her. But it was only due to good luck that she didn't – her father deliberately gave her a lethal dose.

Conveniently, Brown had gone out just before the shooting to give himself the perfect alibi. He went to a nearby store and bought groceries.

When the police arrived at his house hours later, he told them he went out in the middle of the night because his wife and daughter were having a flaming row. He appeared to be a genuinely grief-stricken husband – shaking and crying, but he was also too "scared" to see his wife's body.

Meanwhile, police found Cinnamon in the backyard lying in her own vomit – lucky to be alive.

She was rushed to hospital, where she fully recovered, but she refused to believe that her father had planned to murder her as well. "I was willing to kill Linda because I loved dad," she says. "I didn't want to lose him. I trusted him. Why would he tell me to do something that wasn't right?"

Young Cinnamon – who had been assured by her dad that she wouldn't go to jail – was devastated when she was

187

found guilty and sentenced to life in prison, with possible parole at the age of 25. But for nearly four years she never once implicated her father in the shocking crime. And yet while she rotted in a juvenile jail, Dad began to live it up with the money he got from insurance policies taken out against his wife's death — two of them drawn up weeks before she was killed, making a total of $500,000.

Then he quietly married his secret mistress Patti, and within a year they had a daughter, Heather.

But not even his new wife was safe. After Brown was finally arrested as the murder mastermind, the father of three also plotted to have Patti killed, along with two American district attorneys, Jay Newell and Jeoffrey Robinson. It was Newell who was sure that Cinnamon had not acted alone and visited her in jail, hoping she'd give him the full story. Finally, after five years, she did.

The turning point came when Newell informed her that Brown and Patti had become parents and had been on a wild spending spree. Cinnamon, now 20, was outraged. Feeling badly betrayed, she finally decided to tell shocked detectives the true twisted and terrifying tale.

"I was mad and angry because David and Patti didn't tell me of the affair," Cinnamon wept on the witness stand. "And I felt so hurt because they just left me and it seemed like I was not important to them any more. They killed Linda just as much as me."

She revealed that, months before the killing, the three of them had plotted several murder methods — including pushing Linda from out of a moving van, running her over and hitting her over the head.

"My father told me that I was too young to get into trouble and they'd simply send me to a psychiatrist and then send me home. He made us feel guilty to get us to co-operate," Cinnamon explained when forced to accept the truth — the man she worshipped had used her.

After Cinnamon confessed to the police, Patti also decided to come clean. She, too, gave evidence against

Brown, who was branded a "diabolical manipulator" and a "paranoid liar" by prosecutors.

One of 11 children, Patti grew up in poverty with an alcoholic mother and an older brother who molested her as a small child. Single-handed, her mum Elaine was struggling to bring up her family on welfare payments when con man Brown came into her life. Then in his 20s, the son of a mechanic, he told her that he was dying of cancer and had six months to live. He asked Elaine whether any of her daughters could help clean his house.

And before very long Brown, who had already been married a couple of times, began dating Pam Bailey – Linda and Patti's sister. He soon dumped her for leggy Linda. After getting her mother's signature on a wedding form, they married in Las Vegas when Linda was 17.

Her brother Alan remembers: "David was always a guy who liked being with young girls. That and money were what he was after."

Brown went to a trade school to study computers and picked it up so well that he soon opened his own firm, helping to retrieve lost data. He began to rake in a fortune.

Linda started working for him and soon knew the business as well as he did. Soon the pressure of living and working together took its toll and they divorced, but then got back together again and remarried.

During this time, Brown's young daughter Cinnamon, from a previous marriage, had been living with her mother but then moved in with her father and Linda. Shortly afterwards Patti Bailey, who was 11, moved in as well.

"I felt like I finally had a family," explained Patti, now 22. "I always felt like I was the black sheep at home but David treated me special. He'd go out and buy me clothes and make me feel good about myself.

"David was everything to me. He was my family. If I thought he was going to be taken away that would be like pulling the plug."

She told the packed courtroom that she "wanted to keep

David to myself". And she was so completely under his spell that it was not hard for her to believe that her sister planned to steal his business.

Admitting that she had helped to kill in order to "protect David", she was sentenced to three years in a reform school.

When Brown was finally arrested in 1988, he wrote dozens of letters to both Patti and Cinnamon begging them not to testify against him, saying that he'd kill himself if he was convicted. He told his daughter: "I can't survive in jail. Don't tell them the whole truth. I would kill myself before I let myself die a slow and painful death in a cell."

And to Patti he wrote: "You should know that neither one of us has bad things to say about the other – only good. We can have our trial together if you want."

When his pleas didn't work, he even planned to have Patti assassinated in jail. When he was behind bars he got friendly with burly convict Richard Steinhart and hired him to get rid of Patti, as well as the two district attorneys Newell and Robinson. But another inmate overheard them plotting and he went to the authorities with the gruesome tale.

Steinhart was then persuaded to wear a hidden tape-recorder, and hours of conversation between him and Brown were recorded. The police also recorded Brown's chat with a policewoman posing as an inmate from Patti's prison. His plan was to pay the "prisoner" to come forward after Patti's death to say that Patti had admitted to her that she'd made up the story against him. "I'll take care of you," he promised the undercover officer. "I do take care of people – that's how I get ahead."

At his arrest Brown claimed that the murder plot was "all just a joke". He said, "It was meant to be a game. I was shocked Linda was killed."

But the tapes were enough to convince the jury that Brown was the brains behind the murder. They took just seven hours to find him guilty. While Cinnamon is set to be freed in a deal worked out with prosecutors, Brown, who's now 37, faces the death penalty or jail for life.

Linda's brother Alan hopes Brown "rots in jail for the rest of his life". But the victim's 59-year-old mother, Elaine, wants a more severe sentence than that. "He took my daughter's life. I want him to hang," she says.

36

Cindy's Candlelit Christmas Dinner Was Never Meant to Be

Christmas is a time for living and giving, and for pretty blonde newly-wed Cindy Apelt, that was exactly what she planned to do. She carefully wrapped her thoughtfully chosen presents for her husband in red ribbons and bows, and laid them out under their huge, lavishly decorated tree.

Cindy, 30, was eagerly anticipating the very romantic candlelit Christmas dinner at an exclusive restaurant that she'd planned with hunky husband Michael, the dashing young German millionaire she had married after their whirlwind three-week courtship. They had been married for 56 blissful days, and now, thought Cindy, they would share a truly memorable Christmas together.

But on Christmas Eve, Cindy's horrifically mutilated body was found 200 yards from the road in the Arizona desert. She had been brutally murdered − stabbed five times, her throat savagely slashed from ear to ear, and her lovely face gruesomely stamped on by her vicious killer in an attempt to make her body unrecognisable.

Festivities were over, for Cindy, her horrified family, and for her distraught husband Michael, who was inconsolable when told the tragic news.

Back at her elegant flat, police began the task of piecing together the seemingly meaningless killing. They found several expensive presents for Cindy's smooth-talking husband, but strangely there was not one − not even a stocking filler − from him to her. It was the first of several clues that finally led police in the dusty town of Mesa, Arizona, to suspect the blond 6ft 7in hulk and his equally striking brother Rudi of the callous killing.

And the most incriminating evidence against Michael, 26, was the fact that Cindy, at his insistence, had taken out a life insurance policy for a staggering $400,000. It cost her $305 a month, an amount she could ill afford on her meagre $10,000-a-year earnings, which is all her work as a nutritionist and part-time waitress brought in. But why would Michael or Rudi, 30, need the money? After all, they had boasted they were worth millions. But an investigation by Interpol showed they had extensive criminal backgrounds and had also both served prison sentences.

The Apelt brothers came to San Diego in August 1988, with Rudi's wife Suzanne and also Anke Dorn, a glam 27-year-old hairdresser who'd been a lover of them both. They toured California and Mexico before arriving in Arizona, where they convinced everyone they were stinking rich.

Sultry Cindy Monkman was swept off her feet by Michael when she met the pair at the hottest nightclub in Mesa. Dripping with gold jewellery, they bragged about their wealth, saying they were international bankers. Cindy's sister, Kathy, recalls: "Michael was a Casanova. He was playing the right game and saying all the right things. He was putting his hands all over Cindy, telling her, 'You're the woman of my dreams.' "

Cindy's friend Annette Clay fell head over heels for Rudi, which meant they were soon going out on foursomes together. But Annette became suspicious of smoothie Rudi's line of patter and talked Cindy into following them home one night. The brothers claimed they were staying at a ritzy hotel, but the girls trailed them to a cheap motel, and when Annette knocked on the door, Anke Dorn answered. A fight erupted, with the girls demanding to know just who the mystery woman was and why the two brothers had lied.

Brunette Annette carried on: "The next day Rudi started screaming at me, calling us stupid and saying that he and his brother had lost their well-paid jobs because their security cover was blown. We were absolutely convinced by them.

Michael Apelt, the murderer.

Brother, Rudi Apelt.

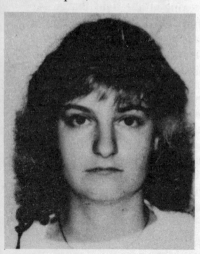

Anke Dorn, hairdresser lover of both brothers.

Cindy Apelt, the victim.

We even felt responsible.'' They even believed the brothers' line that they were financially supporting Anke while her husband was in a nearby hospital. So, as besotted as ever, and just 20 days after they met, Cindy married Michael in Las Vegas.

At 2am on Christmas Eve, Michael called the cops to report that his wife had got a mysterious phone call earlier that evening and had rushed out, saying only she could handle it. Cindy allegedly told her husband she'd meet him for a romantic dinner later, but hadn't been seen since.

Two weeks after Cindy's body was found, the Apelts, along with Anke, were hauled in for questioning. Under an intense grilling, Anke broke down and admitted Michael had murdered Cindy for the insurance money, while Rudi stood guard.

A bloodstained pillowcase and a receipt from a knife shop were both found in Michael's flat. And although he claimed he was at home when she disappeared, a camera situated at an automatic bank machine recorded his picture at the time.

After a 17-month investigation, it took a jury seven hours to convict him of first-degree murder. Saying that ''This was a cold-blooded murder,'' Judge Robert Dean then sentenced Michael to die in the gas chamber. His brother was found guilty at a second trial and is still awaiting sentence. Now Germany, which is firmly opposed to the death penalty, wants the Apelts extradited to serve their sentence in Germany.

But for Cindy's grief-stricken family, there is no escape from the horror of her murder. ''Nothing can make anything right,'' sobbed her sister Kathy. ''Christmas won't ever be the same without Cindy.''

37

A Deadly Obsession

The killer sprang out of the shadows as dishy mum Dianne Hood was leaving a meeting for victims of a deadly rare disease. Wearing a ski mask, gloves and heavy army fatigues, the gunman attempted to wrestle Dianne's purse from her and then shot her in the chest at point-blank range. As her friends watched in horror, Dianne tried to run for safety while screaming for help. But the bandit chased her down the street and fired two more shots into her back. While the mother of three lay on the ground bleeding to death, the cruel killer grabbed her purse and fled into the night.

A few hundred yards away, the pint-sized gunman frantically pulled off the camouflaged clothes and threw them into a park rubbish bin. And then, as the murderer ripped off the black ski mask, her beautiful blonde hair suddenly cascaded down her back. Her gloves came off next, revealing her slender, long fingers and beautifully polished nails. Breathing heavily, her ample bosom pounded against her tight sweater as she made a quick phone call, then jumped into her car and drove home to tuck her kids into bed.

The cold-blooded murder led to a state of panic in the small town of Colorado Springs, with fears that a thrill-killing madman was on the loose. Terrified women refused to go out, believing he'd soon strike again, while police were flooded with calls from people reporting suspicious noises or strangers wearing fatigues. But within days, the shocking truth came out and families were able to feel safe once again. Tension eased when it was revealed that the killer was a stunning beauty posing as a man to throw police off the scent of a deadly love triangle.

Dianne's "heartbroken" husband Brian told newsmen the day after the killing: "She was a Christian, and she's at home in heaven now. And she is rejoicing with the Lord." However, in many people's eyes, she's more likely to be turning in her grave.

The chilling case quickly began to unravel when police got a telephone tip that hunky Brian was having an affair with sexy flower-girl Jennifer Reali. She soon confessed to the gruesome murder but pinned the blame on Brian, saying he brainwashed her into doing it. Hood invoked the *Fatal Attraction* defence, claiming she acted entirely on her own. He hoped to convince a jury that she was totally obsessed with him and had convinced herself that his wife was the only thing stopping them from being together forever. Police, however, argued that while she may have done it for love, he did it for the £50,000 insurance policy.

Incredibly, although a mountain of evidence pointed to him plotting the whole thing, his wife's family believed he was the victim of Jenny's deadly obsession. Dianne's brother David Moore said: "I think Brian is innocent. I think everyone in my family thinks he's innocent, and the truth will come out. We're 100 per cent behind him. The cops have based their prosecution on the testimony of a woman whose mental competency hasn't been established. There's some serious doubts."

Brian and Dianne were considered by their closest friends at one time to have a dream life – a perfect marriage, three wonderful children and a comfortable house with a spectacular view of the Colorado mountains. The couple met during a chemistry class at the Angelo State University in Texas, and found that they had a perfect chemistry of their own. "It was love at first sight," he said.

The 6ft 2in well-built athlete was the typical all-American boy. He was a star football player on his university team, while she was the beautiful blonde cheerleader type. After they graduated, they married on 12, December 1980, and moved to Colorado, where he got a job as an insurance agent. While he went to work she was happy to play the dutiful wife and homemaker to their three kids — Jarrod, nine, Leslie, seven, and Joshua, two. But things began going downhill five years ago when she became a born-again Christian. He seemed to follow her spiritual lead and took the family to the Fellowship Bible Church every Sunday. But, on the side, he secretly started performing ungodly acts with dishy Jeannie Deboe.

Admitting she still felt "awfully close" to Brian, Jeannie said: "He wasn't in love with his wife, but he didn't want to get a divorce because he might lose his children, since it was against his wife's beliefs as a Christian." She told a court hearing that he once suggested to her that she should kill Dianne by running her car off the road. But at the time Jeannie didn't think he was serious.

Brian's marriage took another turn for the worse when his 32-year-old wife came down with a sudden mystery illness. She was finally diagnosed as having the sometimes deadly disease called lupus, which weakens internal organs, usually the kidneys, heart and central nervous system. Some patients lead normal lives, but it can cause immense pain of the joints and extreme fatigue. To help get through the suffering, she joined a local women's lupus support group and prayed regularly at home, using a prayer book she kept at her bedside. Outwardly, her husband acted like the devoted husband and father, helping out around the house and looking after the kids. But inwardly he wanted out of the marriage and started having another affair.

To escape from his ailing wife, fitness fanatic Brian regularly went to a local gym, the US Swim and Fitness Club. It was not long before the smooth-talking salesman was pumping iron alongside shapely Jenny Reali, who worked at a nearby florist's shop. They were soon working out regularly together . . . in bed. Right after they became lovers, Brian approached a friend, Michael Maher, about murdering his wife.

Maher said: "He told me that he couldn't kill her, and she couldn't kill herself because he wouldn't get the insurance that way. He said he needed to find a third person to act as a trigger. I didn't think he meant it, but I got real nervous and told him that wasn't the road he should be taking, and that he needed some help. Then I left the room." Maher added that Hood gave him the impression that it would be a mercy killing, because his wife was dying a slow and painful death. But when Maher saw her a week later she showed no signs of the illness.

In August last year, Hood bought a .45 semi-automatic pistol "for protection", from gun dealer Dallas Salladay. He paid for it with gold and silver coins given to him by Jeannie Deboe, whom he was still seeing on the side while supposed to be madly in love with Jenny Reali. Salladay told a court hearing that Hood asked if he had any ski masks. "I said no, and he asked if we had any Halloween masks. I said, 'What are you going to do, rob a bank?' We laughed about that."

The gun that Brian bought was not the one that killed Dianne. Reali used an antique, four-calibre .46 Colt revolver from a valuable gun collection belonging to her husband, army captain Ben Reali. She also borrowed a pair of his old army fatigues and gloves to disguise herself. Her husband, who'd got wind of the affair, became suspicious when she asked him to put the gun in the armoury at Fort Carson because she didn't like it around the house. After he went to the police and forensic tests proved it was the murder weapon, his wife was arrested. They are now separated, and he has custody of their two children.

Reali, 28, claims she was so spellbound by Brian that he was easily able to "brainwash" her into committing the brutal murder. She told police that she'd tried once before to kill Dianne, but could not go through with it. Police detective Steve Wood said, "She told us that Hood was very angry. He accused her of not loving him enough.'' Jenny also alleged that Brian told her he'd made dangerous turns in his car, hoping another vehicle would kill his wife by ramming her side. But he eventually gave up on the idea when he realised he could also be killed.

"He convinced me that it was God's will that his sick wife should die so we could be together," Reali said. The 5ft 5in, 9-stone beauty added that it was his suggestion that she dress up like a man and make it look like a robbery. So at 8.30pm on 12 September, she lay in wait outside the Otis Park Community Centre to ambush Dianne as she left her weekly lupus meeting. That night Dianne pinned a corsage to her jacket to show that she was the hostess for the evening. A couple of hours later it was covered with blood.

Whenever Jenny wanted to talk to Brian, she'd call him and then hang up when someone answered. He'd know to call her back when he had the opportunity. But on the day of the murder, she says the call was their signal that the dirty deed had been done.

Jennifer Reali was sentenced to life, without parole, and Brian Hood was found guilty, but is eligible for parole in 12 years.

38

Lethal Dose

This astonishing picture captures that terrifyingly awful moment when 35-year-old beauty Paula Prince bought her own death. Paula, a pretty blonde air hostess, is paying for a bottle of painkillers at Walgreens drug superstore in Chicago, unaware that the pills are laced with cyanide.

Lurking nearby is James Lewis, the man who holds the key to the murder of Paula and six other victims. Caught on a security camera, he gleefully watches her every move.

Paula had just returned from a three-day, long-distance trip and told a friend she had a splitting headache, so she picked up a pack of Extra-Strength Tylenol capsules. When she got home, Paula called her best friend, 28-year-old Jean Regula, and left a message on her answering machine, saying, "I've some exciting news to tell you." Nobody will ever know what that news was.

She went into the bathroom and took two Tylenol pain-relief capsules for the headache. She had been out of town – and she felt too tired to bother with TV or radio. Otherwise, she might have caught up with the warnings being issued: "If you live in Chicago, don't touch Tylenol."

Two days later, her worried sister, Carol, found her body curled up on the bathroom floor.

Paula Prince was the seventh, and last, person to die from the poisoned pills within 48 excruciating hours. Lewis, now 45, was never charged with the murders because police could not prove he committed them. But he has served eight years in jail for trying to blackmail the manufacturers of Tylenol.

The slaughter started at 6.10am on 29 September, 1982. Schoolgirl Mary Kellerman woke with a runny nose. It was

201

A closed circuit security camera caught James Lewis, then bearded, looking on as victim Paula Prince bought a bottle of cyanide-spiked pain-killers at a drugstore in New York. When she got home, the 35 yr old air hostess took two of the Tylenol Extra-strength pills. Two days later her sister found her body curled up in the bathroom.

Mary McFarland

Paula Prince

Adam Janus

Mary Kellerman

Stanley Janus

Theresa, Stanley's wife.

Above: James Lewis, 45, was jailed for 10 years for blackmail and 10 years for fraud. He's now served the first half of his sentence, but police could not prove murder.

Top: The Illinois Attorney General released this retouched photo showing Theodore Wilson, a.k.a. James Lewis, Robert Richardson and 16 other aliases, with and without a beard.

a bout of flu. "Daddy," she said, "I don't feel so well. Could you give me something to make me feel better, so I can go to school?"

Her father, Dennis, gave her a red and white Tylenol capsule and a glass of water. Within seconds of swallowing the pill, she collapsed. In two hours, she was dead.

That same morning, 27-year-old postal worker Adam Janus had a chest pain. Sitting in the kitchen with his children — Kathy, four, and Tommy, two — he took a pill. By the end of that afternoon, he was dead. When Adam's 25-year-old brother Stanley came to the house with his wife Theresa, 19, to comfort the family, each, unsuspecting, took two Tylenol capsules as a sedative.

Stan collapsed first. And Theresa — baffled and terrified — clutched hold of him. "Don't you die as well!" she screamed.

Then she collapsed. Hospital doctors fought in vain to save the couple.

The next victim was 27-year-old Mary Reiner, who three days earlier had given birth to her fourth baby, Joshua. She complained of an awful migraine and took a Tylenol instead of an aspirin in case it made her breastfed baby sick. Ten minutes later, in front of her horrified children, she had convulsions and was doubled up in agony. Mary quickly slipped into a coma. Within hours she, too, was dead.

That evening, 31-year-old Mary McFarland, divorced mother of two, was working at the Phone Center Store in Lombara, Illinois. She went to the ladies' room to get some water to wash down the Tylenol she was taking for her headache. She didn't come out alive.

By now, the Tylenol connection was being made. A nationwide alert went out. And drug giant Johnson & Johnson, who own the makers of Tylenol, McNeil Consumer Products, tested every bottle in Illinois. In 75 pills, spread among eight containers, cyanide was found.

Tests revealed that the killer, wearing gloves, had taken capsules from each bottle, pulled them apart, emptied out all the contents and replaced them with cyanide crystals. Then he put the pills back on sale.

The FBI launched a massive manhunt for the person who had spiked these popular painkillers. They followed up thousands of leads and questioned 10,000 people. But they found no real clues that could lead them to the killer responsible.

Two weeks later, Tylenol makers McNeil got a blackmail letter saying that if they wanted an end to the cyanide killings, they must wire $1 million to account no 84-49-97 at the Continental Illinois Bank.

But the writer had not bothered to wear gloves. A fingerprint on the letter led police to James Lewis, who was on the run from fraud charges in Missouri.

In 1978, Lewis had also been charged with killing 78-year-old Raymond West and carving up the body. But he had been acquitted of this charge. Lewis — born Theodore Wilson, in Memphis in 1946, had been adopted, with his three sisters, by Lloyd Lewis, who often mistreated him. When Lloyd died, his widow remarried — to a man Lewis hated so much he was twice arrested for beating him up. Eventually Lewis was sent to a mental hospital.

Later he graduated from Missouri University, where he'd met his wife, Leann. He worked as an importer, then a tax consultant . . . and tried to cash in on his clients' accounts.

As the murder hunt went on, Lewis wrote to newspapers from his New York hideout, denying he was the Tylenol killer. Police issued a photograph of him, with the beard, and also an Identikit picture without it.

Two months later, Lewis, a bespectacled six-footer, was spotted in the New York Public Library by one of the staff. After his arrest he revealed that he (wrongly) blamed Johnson & Johnson for the death of his five-year-old daughter, Tony, who had Down's Syndrome and had died after open-heart surgery in 1974. She had been taking a medicine made by the drug company. Families of the poison victims blamed the makers for their own agony — and sued

McNeil. The firm denied negligence, but the case was settled out of court.

Lewis has now done his time on the blackmail charge. He is still serving the consecutive 10-year fraud sentence. But next year, he applies for parole. And, though many are convinced he is a mass killer, he could soon be on the streets again.

"He has committed one of the most heinous crimes in American history," claims US attorney Anton Valukas. "And I believe he is still a very serious danger to the public."

39

Confession of the Killer

Robert and Marilyn Reza were the couple who had it all. During 22 years of a blissful marriage they'd had two lovely daughters. He'd built up a flourishing medical practice where his wife worked at his side. Every Sunday they'd walk arm in arm to the New Life Community Church in New York, where they were respected worshippers.

Only one problem dogged the dashing doctor. How to get rid of his wife so he could be with the woman he secretly loved, church organist Kathy Senese.

The couple had been making sweet music for months and now Romeo Reza wanted his devoted wife out of his life. But he didn't want it to cost him a penny in a divorce settlement.

So he cold-bloodedly hatched a brutal plot to dispose of her. The devious doc bought a rifle and decided to murder her while he was supposed to be 400 miles away at a conference in Washington, DC.

His plan worked and Marilyn, 47, a nurse at Reza's Suffolk County Lung Association Clinic, was found dead in her bed, having been shot through the head and strangled.

Police were quickly on the case, believing it to be a bungled burglary at Reza's $400,000 home. But the "perfect" crime had a fatal flaw and the doctor's alibi soon collapsed.

Reza knew the game was up and admitted the gruesome murder in a 12-page confession. This is how he said he carried out his crime:

"I was so frustrated with my life I decided to buy a gun

L.I. DOC CONFESSES TO WIFE'S MURDER

By DON BRODERICK

A prominent Long Island doctor confessed that he murdered his 47-year-old wife as she slept in their bed, Suffolk County police said.

Dr. Robert Reza, a pulmonary specialist, told police he used a .22-caliber rifle to shoot his wife, Marilyn, then strangled her with a necktie, according to Sgt. Peter Kelly, a police spokesman.

Reza confessed after cops challenged his alibi — that he was in Washington, D.C., at the time murder.

The couple recently began to have marital difficulties, according to Kelly.

Police found the woman's body in the bedroom of her elegant Bayport home on Dec. 12 about 11 a.m. after her co-workers — worried by her absence — alerted a neighbor.

Reza originally told detectives that he had gone to a medical conference in Washington on Dec. 10 and did not return until he was notified of his wife's death.

A nationally prominent pulmonary disease expert, Reza was attending a conference on tuberculosis in Washington when his wife's body was found.

He broke down in tears when he arrived at their home and spoke to police on Dec. 12.

The woman, a registered nurse and well-known member of the community, had last been seen alive by co-workers when she left the Patchogue office of her

TRAGIC COUPLE: *Family photo shows Dr. Robert Reza with his wife, Marilyn, whom he has confessed to murdering.*

husband on Dec. 11.

Detectives were originally baffled by the crime, as there were no signs of forced entry into the house and the burglar alarm had been turned off.

But Reza's alibi fell apart when detectives were unable to verify his account of his whereabouts.

"An investigation revealed Dr. Reza had returned to New York late in the evening of Dec. 11 and returned to Washington in the early morning of Dec. 12," Kelly said.

"With this information the investigation focused on him."

The woman worked as a nurse in her husband's office at the Suffolk County Pulmonary Association in Patchogue.

Another police spokesman, Officer Mark Ryan, said Reza "provided police with an account of the murder" when confronted with the evidence.

Reza told police that he spoke to his wife before they went to bed and waited until she was asleep before shooting her in the head with a .22-caliber rifle.

Ryan said he believed Reza drove home from the conference to kill his wife and then returned several hours later.

Reza is scheduled to be arraigned for second-degree murder today in Suffolk County First District Court in Hauppauge

---

The Victim - The rich Rezas (Robert & Marilyn) appeared the perfect couple to neighbours, but all he wanted to do was to get rid of her and avoid a costly divorce settlement.

and kill Marilyn. But I didn't know anything about guns so I contacted a church member who was into them. He took me shooting and I asked him what would be a good gun to use to shoot indoors. He said a .22 rifle.

"I discussed buying one with Marilyn and we ended up arguing. She didn't want a gun in the house, but I told her it was only fair for me to buy myself a Christmas present as she was getting an exercise bicycle.

"She gave in and I bought a pump-action rifle for about $370. When Marilyn saw the gun she didn't like it and wanted me to change it for another, but I didn't.

"I wrapped the rifle in red Christmas paper and put it away in a closet in the attic. Later I secretly took it out, ripped off the paper and hid it behind a filing cabinet in my daughter's room so that it would be easy to get hold of when I came home the next week to kill Marilyn.

"I was due to go away to a medical conference for four days that week and had already decided it would provide a good cover for the murder. When I picked up my plane tickets I bought an extra one but paid cash. I showed the travel agent a credit card for identification and he wrote Mr R. Reza on the ticket.

"I hadn't set a definite date to kill Marilyn during the week. I decided I would play it day by day while I was away and see how it worked out. On the day I left, we had breakfast together before I drove to the airport to fly to Washington. The morning after I arrived, I woke up and realised that was the day to fly back and kill her.

"I called Marilyn at 7.10pm and she said she was going to make a nice woodsy fire and write Christmas cards. I lay on the bed for 20 minutes to gather my thoughts. This was the best opportunity to commit the murder because it was in between meetings and I had until 10am the next day to get back before being considered missing.

"I took only my briefcase and left my suitcase in the hotel. I put the 'do not disturb' sign on the door of my room so the maids wouldn't go in the next morning. As I walked by the Sizzler restaurant I saw a friend – I don't know if he saw me. I walked to the Metro and went to the airport. I took the 9pm shuttle using the extra ticket. I arrived in New York one hour later and immediately picked up my car from the parking lot.

"I drove directly home and parked in the driveway. I entered by the kitchen door. Marilyn was in the kitchen. It was about 11.05pm. She was wearing street clothes and writing Christmas cards by the fire. She was very surprised to see me when I walked in. But we didn't argue. We chatted briefly and decided to go to bed. She slipped into a nightie and took half a sleeping tablet before turning in. I got in beside her and waited till she dozed off.

"After an hour I was sure the sleeping tablet had taken effect and she was sound asleep. I carefully got up and fetched the rifle from its hiding place. I didn't bother putting the lights on as there was enough illumination from the Christmas candles that she had put in the window.

"The rifle was already loaded and ready to fire. I wanted to kill Marilyn quickly by putting a bullet through her brain. She was sleeping on her back and I just walked up to her side, pointed the gun at her head and pulled the trigger.

"The gun went off with a loud bang and I knew I had killed her. She just lay there completely still. I checked for a pulse but there was nothing. I put the rifle down and quickly dressed in jeans and a shirt – I had to make her death look like a burglary.

"I turned out the drawers and messed up the room. Then, to make it look as if she had been strangled, I fetched a tie and tightened it around her lifeless neck.

"I grabbed the gun, went downstairs and and opened the east side door, and left it ajar to make it look like the point of entry. I left via the kitchen door, taking the gun with me, and drove off in my car with the lights switched off.

"I had to get rid of the gun and drove to a nearby creek. I hurled the rifle over the bridge and then drove back to the airport to leave the car.

"Rather than fly back to Washington again, I caught a cab from the airport to the train station and caught the early morning express. I managed to get back to my hotel at 9.30am before anyone had noticed I had been gone — the 'do not disturb' sign was still on the door.

"I am giving this statement at police headquarters and have read it. I swear it is the truth."

After the killing, Reza coolly continued with the conference until he telephoned his office later in the day, to be told the "tragic" news that his wife was dead.

The devious doctor immediately flew back to New York. When he returned home he was besieged by an army of reporters and camera crews. Standing with his arm around his daughter Elizabeth, 20, for comfort, he told them: "I just want to say this family is in shock." He added he was impressed with what the police were doing.

Reza was even more impressed by the police a week later — when he was arrested! The skilled surgeon was a clumsy murderer. His plan was riddled with holes:

- The rifle he'd tried to hide in the creek was recovered;
- His name was on the ticket for the flight the night of the murder;
- The house's alarm was off, indicating his wife knew the killer.

The clever man was a fool for love. Despite Reza's attempt to protect his lover by leaving her out of his confession, Kathy Senese went to the police and blabbed her part in the grisly saga.

Two days after his arrest, Senese came forward and publicly admitted sleeping with Reza. She said she believed he had killed his wife because of their torrid affair.

It transpired their romance had first blossomed at a wedding when he sat next to Senese. Reza, an elder at the church, had fancied her and slipped her a piece of paper with his phone number on. He told her to ring if she needed anything.

When she did call, she asked for help in getting a pay rise from the church where she had been an organist for 19 years. Reza saw his chance to ingratiate himself and arranged the increase. He then began showering her with gifts. He took her out and encouraged her musical career. After they began having sex she left her husband and kids, expecting him to divorce his wife and marry her — but he had other murderous plans.

He even revealed to her that he'd had a dream that his wife had died. Later he said: "If anything happens to Marilyn, don't feel guilty. I may look distraught but I won't be."

She said: "I believe he killed his wife because he was having an affair with me. Nothing will bring Marilyn back but I'm sorry for the affair."

Bizarrely, Reza, a part-time professor at New York State University, rarely talked to Senese about his wife — except to say that she was perfect!

Relatives and friends were shocked by the savage killing. "It's amazing," said one. "They had a really good relationship." They said Reza had never hinted at any marital problems. Nor did he show any signs of difficulty in coping with success — which he claimed was the motive for the murder.

One longtime business associate, who refused to be named, said he was stunned when he saw the news flashed up on television. "They announced that a woman had been killed in Bayport and I said to my wife: 'I only know one woman there.' Then they said it was Marilyn. My God, I was shocked.

"Then when Robert was arrested we all reacted with disbelief. There were no indications of trouble in the marriage. They worked well together and she loved him. She was a lady. A saint. Marilyn had class and he treated her with respect."

Pastor John Smith, who'd known Marilyn for 10 years, agreed. "In her faith and personal life she came as close to Christian perfection as you can come," he said. "She was a real servant. She helped people out, responded to friends, and nobody would know about it."

Reza is now awaiting trial and faces the rest of his life behind bars.

40

Flashback

At just eight years old, Eileen Franklin watched in stunned horror as her best friend Susie Nason was viciously raped and murdered. The shock locked the macabre scene into the hidden recesses of her mind until, 20 years later, a flashback hammered home the terrible truth. The callous killer of the pretty, freckle-faced, redheaded child was Eileen's own perverted father.

Two years ago Eileen, now 29, looked into the eyes of her five-year-old daughter and found herself back on a roadside, crouching by the family van. Daughter Jessica, who bears a striking resemblance to the victim, turned to look at Eileen. And her sparkling blue eyes suddenly unlocked the horrible truth that Eileen had managed to blank out for so long. She saw the shocking image of a menacing man hovering over little Susie, holding a huge rock above his head. That man, she said, was her father, George Franklin.

And, in a landmark case in California, the wealthy 51-year-old has been sentenced to life imprisonment on her evidence.

The memory of the hideous crime that Eileen had witnessed came flooding back in gory detail. Eileen and Susie had grown up together in Foster City, California, a charming waterfront suburb of San Francisco, and played together virtually every day. But their friendship was tragically cut short on 9 September, 1969, when Susie was last seen walking from her home to a schoolfriend's house. It was only a quarter of a mile trip, but it was long enough for the cruel killer to strike.

Eileen later remembered driving along the road with her father in their Volkswagen camper van. They saw Susie and offered her a lift, and the girls began playing gleefully on a mattress kept in the back of the van.

"We were bouncing around in the back and my father got out," says Eileen. "He climbed in the back and started innocently playing with us. I got into the front passenger seat. Then when I looked round, Susie was on the end of the mattress and my father was holding her hands above her head. He was on top of her, his pelvis against her. Susie's legs were apart. I think she said, 'Stop' and 'Don't'. Next thing I remember, we were outside the van, Susie crouching beside me.

"Then I saw the silhouette of my father with the sun coming up behind him. He had his hands above his head — he was holding a rock. I did something which caused Susie to look up at me. I think I yelled or screamed but I'm not sure. She looked up and met my eyes, then turned her head to look at my father and brought her hands up to cover her head. I turned away. I heard a second blow. Susie's hand caught my eye. She had a ring on her finger and it was smashed in.

"He said, 'It's over now. Forget about it.' He told me I was a part of it as I'd wanted Susie to get in the van, and if I told anyone they'd put me away. He threatened to kill me."

When Eileen got home, she ran straight to her bedroom, terrified and badly shaken. By the time she went back to school after the holidays, she had managed to block out the whole incident. All she could remember was "being unable to function properly, not being able to learn".

Susie's body was discovered by Ephne Bottimore, a caretaker for the local water company, in a ravine two months after the killing. The murder remained unsolved, until Eileen's startling revelations.

At first the adult Eileen, who was seeing a therapist to try to patch up her failing marriage to Barry Lipsker,

Top: The defence of George Franklin (right), pictured here with his attourney, claimed his daughter Eileen made up the grisly accusation. But her regained memory of the murder of Susie was too accurate.

Below: Key witness Eileen, daughter of the accused, approaches court.

thought she was going crazy. But as her memory grew stronger, she eventually told her husband and he took her straight to the police.

When the police investigated George Franklin, they discovered he had paedophile preferences. Eileen's sister Janice, 31, later testified that she'd always suspected her alcoholic father of the murder. She revealed that he'd sexually assaulted both her and Eileen and subjected them to physical and emotional abuse. She'd told police of her suspicions six years earlier, but Franklin had been ruled out because of a mix-up over the time he had been seen that fateful day.

As George Franklin was sentenced, Eileen admitted that, despite the horror, it was still hard for her to hate her own father, and difficult to turn him in. "I don't like the idea of him going to jail," she admits. "I've always loved him and I still have strong feelings for him. But I owe it to Susie to put him away for life."

It's not unusual for a child's mind to blank out all memory of a dreadful experience, says Dr Lenore Tarr. "If something unusual and terrible happens in ordinary life, it would be remembered," she says. "But kids who go through traumatic experiences have a way of saying, 'I'm not seeing.' An intense reminder gets them to recall."

41

Randy Rev Robbed for Lust

Life seemed to be heaven on earth for the Reverend Roy Yanke . . . a very sexy heaven. Because the 27-year-old pastor, who was a pillar of his community, certainly didn't practise what he preached. The randy rev robbed banks to pay for raunchy romps with call girls.

This man of the cloth enjoyed the pleasures of the flesh so much he stole more than $25,000 from 14 banks to satisfy his appetite for sex — and none of his parishioners ever guessed he was the Bearded Bandit terrorising their local banks.

"I wish I could say the Reverend Yanke spent all the money that he stole from the banks on his church," says shocked FBI agent John Anthony. "But he told us he spent it on illicit sex — from local street prostitutes to high-class hookers. He admitted he just had to satisfy his enormous appetite for sex."

At least four times a week, the Rev Yanke would visit call girls in the wealthy town of Beverly Hills, Michigan. Sometimes he picked up a girl twice in one day — and all the time, Yanke was still making love regularly to his poor, unsuspecting wife Deborah. But while he was out supposedly doing God's work among his wealthy flock, the sex-crazed vicar of the Covenant Alliance Church was frolicking in seedy motels with hookers he found through a sleazy telephone escort service.

Now, wife Deborah is terrified her husband may have caught AIDS and passed it on to her . . . but incredibly she's sticking by him. And so are his parishioners.

"I understand Yanke's wife is very worried about catching

AIDS," says police chief William Dwyer, who investigated the bank raids. Even so, on the Sunday after Yanke was arrested, his wife tenderly nestled her head on his shoulder as they sang hymns with the congregation. Then she thanked members of her husband's church for their support.

"We're both overwhelmed by the expressions of love we've received from people in our community – our friends, our family and much-loved congregation," she said, between tears. "We're deeply grateful and ask that everyone will continue to pray for us in the days ahead."

Nevertheless, the rich community was stunned by the scandal. Despite the fact Yanke had given hundreds of sermons attacking sinners during his eight years with the church, he was one of those who'd fallen.

The police and the FBI, too, were shocked when they collared the villain known as the Bearded Bank Bandit and discovered he was a holy man.

The respected reverend's double life began in September 1989 when he robbed a small bank just three doors away from his church. Says FBI agent Anthony, "In each robbery, the Bearded Bandit walked up to the terrified teller, passed them a large manila envelope and a handwritten note demanding money." Although he only once showed a weapon, he kept one hand in his pocket to make it look like he carried a gun.

Anthony says Yanke disguised himself slightly by dyeing his hair red and wearing make-up to darken his skin. He also painted a scar on his face and sometimes wore glasses. He was often caught on the bank's video cameras – but what gave his holy terror game away were his getaway cars.

Several witnesses noted his number plates, and the cars were traced by a local rental company who then revealed the hirer was none other than the local vicar. On his last robbery Rev Yanke calmly parked the car in the church car park, where it was discovered by the police.

"He matched the description of our bandit to a T," says

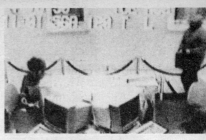

Bearded bandit exposed. Secret cameras caught Rev Roy Yanke as he passed tellers his demands before heading off in search of sex and fun from his wicked gains.

Top: Sin City...the minister sometimes picked up two prostitutes in one day. 'He had to satisfy his tremendous appetite for sex' says an FBI agent.

Above: Covenant Alliance Church.

an officer. Yanke, who has a 10-year-old daughter Heather and is active in the local Parent Teacher Association, was charged with robbing one bank of about $500 and another of $700. Then he admitted he was the stick-up man at 12 other banks in the area. The minister had netted around $25,000 and had blown the lot on his sex habit, which cost him up to $75 an hour or $10 for a briefer encounter. He'd also just taken out a $7,500 loan on his house, leading police to believe his addiction to sex had already decimated his family savings.

The reverend resigned from his pulpit − but continued going to Sunday services. In the first week after his arrest, the church elder Alex Hoover made it clear he should be forgiven for his sins of the flesh.

"Brothers, if someone is caught in a sin, restore them gently," he told the close-knit congregation. "I think it would be wholesome for our church, for those of you led by the Lord to stand and acknowledge that you have the spirit of forgiveness for the ones who really need it."

Along with many others in his flock, the Rev Yanke wept quietly while his wife sobbed aloud. For 40 minutes after the service the 130-strong congregation gathered round to hug the couple. "Roy knows he's loved here," said one. "It's probably the best place for him to come."

Yanke's friends at the nearby William Beaumont Hospital, where as chaplain he'd often comforted the sick and the dying, were also shocked at the not-so-reverent revelations. Nobody had suspected their kind-hearted minister of such seedy hanky-panky − and it seems that's why most people are sticking by him and blaming darker forces for his sordid deeds.

"This is the Devil's work," says one churchgoer, June Badder. "I'm sure that's what's behind it − the Devil. This doesn't change what we stand for. Men fail. God doesn't."

Fellow pastor the Rev John Steiner immediately sprung to Yanke's defence, saying, "He's an impeccable citizen, a good minister and a very good father." Yanke's neighbour adds, "I still can't believe it. He seemed a nice, quiet person."

Many experts are saying that Yanke's antics suggest he wanted to be caught so he could get help for his sex habit. They think a church minister who robs banks without a mask and spends the loot on prostitutes is crying out for help.

Dr Paul Schubert says: "Sometimes, ministers will take risks when they're really calling for help — and do something shameful to contrast with their expected role in society." He says renting getaway cars and driving them to church were signs Yanke wanted to be caught.

"Most people aren't aware of the pressures ministers are under and the expectations they live with." He reveals that Yanke's sex habit could've been caused by deep emotional problems. "A sex addiction can mean there are unfulfilled personal needs acted out sexually."

Yanke was sentenced to seven years in jail and must repay $37,500. "God be with him," says the ever loyal and forgiving church elder.